THE FRENCH CHEESE GUIDE

*ISBN: 979-10-301-0201-7
Legal deposit: May 2017
Printed and bound in Spain*

*Tana éditions, un département d'Édi8
12, avenue d'Italie
75013 Paris
Tél. : 01 44 16 09 00
Fax : 01 44 16 09 01
www.tana.fr*

Julie Soucail
Photographs: Louis-Laurent Grandadam

THE FRENCH CHEESE GUIDE

The essential guide

Production – degustation – wine pairing

Tana
éditions

CONTENTS

VEINED CHEESES

REGION
Auvergne

MILK AND FEEDING
Raw cow's milk. Cows: any breed. Fodder from the designation zone and pasture grazing.

APPEARANCE
Semi-firm, ivory in colour, crumbly, tender and creamy; even, blue marbling.

TASTE AND FLAVOUR
Assertive and persistent parsley taste, flavours of undergrowth and wild mushrooms.

ACCOMPANIMENTS
Sourdough bread, rye bread, country ham, dried fruits (nuts, cashews); sweet flavours: fresh fruit (pear, date, gooseberrie), gingerbread.

WINES
Sweet whites (chenin): montlouis, vouvray. If you don't like white wine, then a Loire red will do (cabernet franc).

AOC/AOP : 1975/1996

BLEU D'AUVERGNE

IT IS ANTOINE ROUSSEL, A NATIVE OF AUVERGNE, TO WHOM WE OWE THE INVENTION OF THE BLEU D'AUVERGNE. HE DEVELOPED A PARTICULAR TECHNIQUE TO CULTURE AND THEN ISOLATE THE RYE BREAD MOULD. FROM THIS CULTURE WAS BORN THE 'BLUE CHEESE POWDER', WHICH WAS ASSOCIATED WITH THE USE OF NEEDLES TO SEED THE CHEESES, HOMOGENISING THE FERMENTATION AND, IN TURN, STABILISED THE PRODUCTION PROCESS AND QUALITY OF THE BLEU D'AUVERGNE. TODAY, ONLY THE ACTIVE INGREDIENT *(PENICILLIUM ROQUEFORTI)* OF THIS POWDER IS STILL IN USE.

UNLIKE ROQUEFORT, THE BLEU D'AUVERGNE IS MADE FROM COW'S MILK, ITS FINAL TEXTURE MORE FIRM AND MOIST RATHER THAN CRUMBLY.

THE VOLCANIC SOIL WHERE THE PRODUCTION OF THIS CHEESE TAKES PLACE GIVES IT ITS SLIGHTLY MINERAL, SELF-ASSURED TASTE. IT RECEIVED THE AOC IN 1975.

STEPS OF PRODUCTION
In contrast to Roquefort, the milk is first seeded with Penicillium roqueforti and then heated and curdled. The curd is then cut into small chunks that are stewed allowing for proper development of the blue mould. After having been cast then drained again, the cheese is salted manually and then pricked with long needles. Maturation in the cellar takes around 4 weeks.

CUTTING

Triangular slices, from the centre, out to the edge.

BEST TASTING PERIOD
April to November.

SERVING
Room temperature (around 20 °C) remove from the refrigerator 1 hour before serving.

STORAGE
Between 2 and 8 ° C, in the crisper of the refrigerator, in its original packaging.

REGION

Aveyron, Lozère and Lot, aged in Aveyron.

MILK AND FEEDING

Whole cow's milk. Cows: any breed. Fodder in winter, including hay and pasture grazing (120 days minimum).

APPEARANCE

White to ivory in colour, depending on the season, dark blue-green veins, creamy, buttery texture.

TASTE AND FLAVOUR
Soft to strong, according to the length of maturation and season, possible bitterness, characteristic blue flavour.

ACCOMPANIMENTS
White bread, fig or apricot bread, toasted gingerbread, dried or fresh fruits: pear, fig, apple; almond or hazelnut.

WINES
White or red wines containing sugar pair naturally. Let your self be tempted by a banuyls, a late harvest pinot gris or gewurztraminer, or even a bonnezeaux.

AOC/AOP : 1991/2009

BLEU DES CAUSSES

FORMERLY BLEU DE L'AVEYRON, THIS MARBLED CHEESE WITH A MOULD CORE OWES ITS CURRENT NAME TO THE NATURAL CAVES IN THE LIMESTONE SLOPES OF THE MASSIF CENTRAL: THE CAUSSES MOUNTAINS. IN THE COOL AND MOIST CAVES, VENTILATED BY 'FLEURINES' (SMALL CAVITIES), THIS CHEESE IS AGED FOR 70 DAYS.

A COUSIN OF THE ROQUEFORT, THOUGH PRODUCED FROM COW'S MILK, ITS SHAPE AND PRODUCTION STYLE ARE SIMILAR.

IT OWES THE SPECIFICITY OF ITS FLAVOURS TO THE WILD VEGETATION, POOR YET VERY FLAVOURFUL, OF THE MOORS OF THE CAUSSES.

DURING THE MATURATION, THE CHEESE IS 'SEALED', MEANING IT IS WRAPPED IN ALUMINIUM FOIL IN ORDER TO PRESERVE ITS CREAMINESS AND ITS UNIQUE FLAVOURS.

STEPS OF PRODUCTION
Seeding of milk with Penicillium roqueforti, rennet added then curdling, cutting into chunks then brewing in order to obtain the "styling" of the chunky curdle. Moulding, draining and salting by hand. Blues are then brushed and pricked through in order to ensure the growth of the Penicillium. Aging for 70 days in natural caves then ripening.

CUTTING

Triangular slices, from the centre out to the edge.

BEST TASTING PERIOD
April to December.

SERVING
Allow to sit at room temperature for 1 hour before tasting.

STORAGE
In its original packaging in the crisper.

REGION
Franche-Comté, Haut-Jura

MILK AND FEEDING
Raw cow's milk. Cows: Montbéliarde or Simmental. Prairie forages in the designation area, pasture grazing.

APPEARANCE
Yellow crust, sometimes mottled with red. Whitish to ivory core, very creamy texture, sometimes crumbly, pale blue-green veins spread throughout.

TASTE AND FLAVOUR
Salty taste, lightly bitter, milky flavour, hints of hazelnut and mushrooms.

ACCOMPANIMENTS
Lamb's lettuce, breads with sweet flavours like sourdough or Vienna bread.

WINES
Head towards a côtes-du-jura or an arbois straw wine (chardonnay or savagnin). A sweet wine from another region would work as well.

AOC/AOP : 1977/1996

BLEU DE GEX

THIS BLUE CHEESE, ALSO CALLED BLEU DE SEPTMONCEL OR BLEU DE GEX HAUT-JURA, OWES THE RICHNESS OF ITS FLAVOURS TO THE FLORA OF THE PASTURES OF THE HAUT-JURA AND ITS MANUAL PRODUCTION TECHNIQUES.

THE FAVOURITE CHEESE OF CHARLES QUINT (16TH CENTURY), RULER OF THE FRANCHE-COMTÉ, THE BLEU DE GEX IS A SWEET BLUE, WITH A LITTLE SALTINESS, IMPORTED BY THE PEASANTS OF THE DAUPHINOIS OF THE SOUTHEAST OF FRANCE, THEN LATER DEVELOPED BY THE MONKS OF THE ABBEY SAINT-CLAUDE.

DURING ITS MATURATION ON SPRUCE PLANKS, IT IS, LIKE ALL OTHER BLUES, PRICKED WITH LONG NEEDLES IN ORDER TO ENSURE AN EVEN MARBLING IN THE CORE.

ITS SPECIFICATIONS REQUIRE A LIMITED ZONE OF PRODUCTION, MAKING THE BLEU DE GEX A RELATIVELY RARE FIND ON MOST SHELVES.

STEPS OF PRODUCTION
Coagulation (rennet) then seeding (penicillium roqueforti), slicing of the curd, brewing, casting, draining through flipping then it is released from the mould before salting with dry salt. Maturation in a cold and moist cellar from 21 to 28 days, pricking occurs between the 7th and 15th day.

CUTTING

Triangular slices, from the centre out to the edge.

BEST TASTING PERIOD
April to November.

SERVING
Room temperature, remove from the refrigerator 1 hour before tasting.

STORAGE
Wrapped in its original paper, at the bottom of the refrigerator.

REGION
Auvergne, Puy-de-Dôme, Cantal, Haute-Loire.

MILK AND FEEDING
Raw cow's milk.
Cows: any breed from the designation area. Forage in the designation area, pasture grazing (150 days minimum).

APPEARANCE
Ivory in colour, veined with blue, soft and creamy consistency; light grey to grey crust.

TASTE AND FLAVOUR
Sweet taste, all with a rounded, fine and fruity body and light hints of bitterness, delicate creamy flavours or undergrowth.

ACCOMPANIMENTS
Baguette, country-style bread, rye or gingerbread; dried fruit (nut, hazelnut, raisin, fig); fresh fruit: berries, mangoes, fresh figs, apples, pears.

WINES
A naturally sweet red, like banuyls or port. You can also give sweet whites a try, like an Alsatian gewurztraminer or a late-harvest pinot gris or a sweet vouvray.

AOC/AOP : 1972/1996

FOURME D'AMBERT

THE MILDEST OF THE VEINED CHEESES, IT IS ALSO ONE OF THE OLDEST IN FRANCE - ITS ORIGINS DATING BACK TO THE TIME OF THE GALLIC DRUIDS. THE MILK COLLECTED FROM FARMS IN MID-RANGE ALTITUDES, BETWEEN 600 AND 1,600 METERS HIGH, GIVES IT A SUBTLE AND DELICATE AROMA.

ITS COMPLEX PRODUCTION INVOLVES A UNIQUE STEP, THE "STYLING" OF THE CURD CHUNKS OBTAINED THROUGH A PAINSTAKING BREWING PHASE. THIS STEP REQUIRES AN AERATION PERIOD FOR AN OPTIMAL FERMENTATION.

IT IS IMPORTANT TO NOTE THAT TODAY ONLY 4 PRODUCTION LOCATIONS IN THE REGION HOLD THE FARMER CERTIFICATION.

STEPS OF PRODUCTION
Aging of the milk then seeding with Penicillium roqueforti, curdling with added rennet, slicing into small chunks before brewing, moulding, draining and salting by hand. The fourmes are then pricked piece by piece for the proper development of the blue. Aged for a minimum of 28 days.

CUTTING
Into pieces.

BEST TASTING PERIOD
April to December.

SERVING
Allow to sit at room temperature for 1 hour before tasting.

STORAGE
In its original packaging in the crisper.

REGION
Île-de-France (Rambouillet).

MILK AND FEEDING
Raw or pasteurized goat's milk. Cows: all types. Fodder.

APPEARANCE
Smooth and melting, white marbled with blue; grey crust.

TASTE AND FLAVOUR
Little salty, lactic, caprine, persistent flavours.

ACCOMPANIMENTS
Sourdough bread, dried fruit bread, pear, fig, apple, quince paste, Muscat grape, almond, hazelnut, honey, mash.

WINES
A white from Loire with chenin cépage: montlouis, vouvray, anjou, savennières. Or try a white from the South of France: côteaux-du-languedoc, hermitage.

AOC/AOP: NONE

PERSILLÉ DE CHÈVRE

THE PERSILLÉ DE CHÈVRE IS A BLUE CHEESE MADE FROM GOAT'S MILK.

ITS TEXTURE IS SMOOTH AND MELTING, ITS WHITE INTERIOR IS MOTTLED WITH BLUE, ITS ASH CRUST, SLIGHTLY MOIST AND BRINGS TO MIND THE TRADITIONAL GOAT CHEESES.

IT IS A RECENTLY INVENTED CHEESE, CREATED IN THE YVELINES, DISTINGUISHED IN 2014 WITH A SILVER MEDAL IN THE GENERAL AGRICULTURAL COMPETITION.

STEPS OF PRODUCTION
Coagulation by adding rennet, slicing of the curd, stirring and then casting. 3-day drainage, manual salting with dry salts, seeding of Penicillium roqueforti, pricking of the dough (development of the moulds) and then covering with vegetable charcoal. Aging from 40 to 90 days.

CUTTING

In triangular slices, from center to edge.

BEST TASTING PERIOD
Year-round.

SERVING
At room temperature, remove it from the refrigerator 1 hour before tasting.

STORAGE
In the refrigerator's crisper, packaged in its original paper.

REGION
For milk: Aude, Aveyron, Gard...
Maturation : takes place in Roquefort-sur-Soulzon in the Aveyron.

MILK AND FEEDING
Raw sheep milk.
Sheep: Lacaune.
Grass and forage taken 75% from the designation area and grains.

APPEARANCE
White to ivory in colour, crumbly, runny, creamy and moist, veined in blue and green.

TASTE AND FLAVOUR
Fine taste, strong flavour, acidic and long in the mouth.

ACCOMPANIMENTS
Country-style bread, rye, white grape, pear, nut, endive, lamb's lettuce, sticks of celery.

WINES
The pairing with a sweet white like sauternes, côteaux-du-layon, is marvellous. Also go for naturally sweet wines like muscat cépage.

AOC/AOP : 1925/1996

ROQUEFORT

FAVOURITE CHEESE OF EMPEROR CHARLEMAGNE AND DISTINGUISHED AS "THE FIRST CHEESE OF EUROPE" FROM 1792 IN *THE ENCYCLOPAEDIA* OF DIDEROT AND D'ALEMBERT, ROQUEFORT HAS THE UNIQUE QUALITY OF BEING DEVELOPED ON A COMPLETELY NATURAL TERRITORY. CAVES BUILT DIRECTLY INTO THE ROCK AND VENTILATED BY FAULTS CALLED "FLEURINES" ASSURES AN IDEAL DEVELOPMENT OF THE *PENICILLIUM ROQUEFORTI*, THIS MICROSCOPIC CHAMPION THAT GIVES IT THIS MARBLED ASPECT IN BLUE AND GREEN, AS WELL AS ITS VERY UNIQUE TEXTURE AND TASTE. THE TOWN OF ROQUEFORT HOLDS A MONOPOLY ON ITS PRODUCTION SINCE THE 15TH CENTURY. IT IS THE CHEESE TO HOLD THE LONGEST STANDING APPELLATION OF ORIGIN, GIVEN IN 1925.

THE LEGEND HOLDS THAT IT WAS BORN FROM A BIT OF SHEEP CHEESE ABANDONED IN A CELLAR IN CAMBALOU BY A SMITTEN SHEPHERD.

STEPS OF PRODUCTION
The milk is first heated to around 30 °C then curdled with the addition of rennet. The curd is then sliced and brewed then moulded. After 3 days of draining, the cheese is salted by hand then seeded with Penicillium roqueforti and several holes are pierced in its body to help the growth of mould. Then comes the maturation lasting 3 weeks in natural caves. The cheeses are then wrapped in tin sheets to continue the maturation for up to 90 days total.

CUTTING

Triangular slices, from the centre to the edge.

BEST TASTING PERIOD
Mars to December.

SERVING
Room temperature (20 °C), remove from refrigerator 1 hour before serving. To be eaten all year long. From April to October, the best of its flavours come out. Avoid sudden changes in temperature; only remove the quantity to be served, leaving the rest in the refrigerator until it is ready to be consumed.

STORAGE
Around 8 °C, in the crisper of the refrigerator, in its original packaging.

SOFT CHEESES WITH MOULD CRUST

REGION
Île-de-France.

MILK AND FEEDING
Raw cow's milk, whole.
Cows: All types.
Fodder and pasture grazing.

APPEARANCE
Firm, pale yellow to butter yellow, soft and shiny; Fluffy crust dotted with black peppercorns.

TASTE AND FLAVOUR
Salty, pronounced and spicy.

ACCOMPANIMENTS
Country bread, baguette, apple, white grape, cucumber, walnut.

WINES
A red with some density: saint-émilion, graves, médoc (merlot, cabernet-sauvignon, cabernet franc).

AOC/AOP: NONE

BRIE AU POIVRE

PRODUCED IN ÎLE-DE-FRANCE AND CLOSE COUSIN OF THE BRIE DE MEAUX, ITS SLOW COAGULATION BASED ON LACTIC FERMENTS, AS WELL AS ITS 8-WEEK RIPENING GIVE IT A FIRMER INTERIOR.

THE GRAINS OF BLACK PEPPER THAT ENCIRCLE ITS CRUST DURING RIPENING GIVE IT A MORE FULL-BODIED FLAVOUR.

IT IS DELICIOUS WHEN MELTED IN THE OVEN ON A SLICE OF BREAD.

STEPS OF PRODUCTION
Slow curdling (lactic ferments), slicing of the curd and hand-moulding with Brie shovel, draining, individual salting with dry salts; Minimum 8 weeks maturing: pre-ripening in hâloir (dryer) between 8 and 16 ° C and maturing in cellars between 4 and 14 ° C. Pepper is added after 5 days of ripening when the cheese is half-fresh.

CUTTING

Sliced, from crust to heart.

BEST TASTING PERIOD
March to December; Optimum season: April to September.

SERVING
Prefer a slightly cool temperature for tasting, remove from refrigerator 30 minutes before tasting.

STORAGE
In its original packaging or in paraffin or parchment paper.

REGION
Île-de-France

MILK AND FEEDING
Raw cow's milk, whole.
Cow: all breeds.
Fodder and pasture grazing.

APPEARANCE
Pale yellow to butter-yellow. From chalky to soft or runny depending on maturity; red-streaked or mottled crust that is floral and fine.

TASTE AND FLAVOUR
Butter, cream, notes of hazelnut, wet leaves, wild mushrooms.

ACCOMPANIMENTS
Country-style bread, raison or fig bread.

WINES
The brie de Meaux is eaten with a dry red: beaujolais (gamay), saint-nicolas-de-bourgueil et chinon (cabernet franc), pinot noir from Alsace or Burgundy.

AOC/AOP : 1980/1996

BRIE DE MEAUX

CROWNED KING OF CHEESES BY TALLEYRAND DURING THE CLOSING BANQUET AT THE CONGRESS OF VIENNA IN 1815, BRIE WOULD HAVE ALREADY BEEN ON THE MENU IN CHARLEMAGNE'S COURT.

PRODUCED ONLY 50 KM FROM PARIS, IT IS ONE OF THE JEWELS OF FRENCH CHEESE PRODUCTION - ITS FINENESS AND SPECIFIC FLAVOURS OF HAZELNUT HAVE EARNED IT THE DESIGNATION OF THE "PASTRY OF CHEESES".

SINCE THE 12TH CENTURY, THE BRIE DE MEAUX IS MOULDED BY HAND, USING THE SAME TOOL TO THIS DAY - THE BRIE SHOVEL. EACH CHEESE IS SALTED DRY BY HAND.

THE BRIE DE MEAUX (AOP) REQUIRES A SLOW MATURATION AT A SPECIFIC TEMPERATURE AND HUMIDITY LEVEL.

STEPS OF PRODUCTION
Curdling (lactic acids and rennet), slicing of the curd, then manual moulding with a brie shovel, draining, individual salting with dry salt; maturation of 4 to 8 weeks: pre-maturation in an hâloir (dryer) between 8 and 16 °C then maturation in a cellar between 4 and 14 °C, humidity between 80 and 98%.

CUTTING

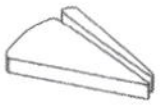

In slices, from the crust to the heart.

BEST TASTING PERIOD
March to December; best season: April to September.

SERVING
A slightly chillier temperature is suggested; remove from refrigerator 30 minutes before serving.

STORAGE
Original packaging or wax or parchment paper.

REGION
Île-de-France, Seine-et-Marne, a part of Aube and Yonne.

MILK AND FEEDING
Raw cow's milk. Cows: 80% from the production site itself or from the geographic designation area. Fodder and pasture grazing.

APPEARANCE
Muted white, fine crust, streaked or mottled with red or brown. Crumbly and slightly runny when young, soft and runny with age.

TASTE AND FLAVOUR
Salty taste, complex flavours, predominantly lactic; milky and slightly acid when fresh; very fruity with age; persistent flavours.

ACCOMPANIMENTS
Country-style bread, green apple, pear, apricot, fig, nut, pine nut, black truffle, basil.

WINES
A light, dry red: arbois rouge (poulsard, trousseau), beaujolais (gamay) or an Alsatian pinot noir.

AOC/AOP : 1980/1996

BRIE DE MELUN

THIS IS CERTAINLY THE FOREFATHER OF ALL OTHER BRIES. ITS TEXTURE IS SOFT AND SHINY, ITS FLAVOURS MORE PRONOUNCED AND IT PRODUCES A STRONG EARTHY ODOUR.

ITS UNIQUENESS IS DUE TO A SLOW FERMENTATION AND TO A SLOW AND UNASSISTED DRAINING. ACCORDING TO THE BROTHERHOOD OF THE BRIE DE MELUN, IT IS THIS CHEESE THAT THE RAVEN FROM THE FAMOUS FABLE BY JEAN DE LA FONTAINE, *THE FOX AND THE RAVEN*, HELD IN ITS BEAK. LIKE THE BRIE DE MEAUX, IT IS SUBJECTED TO A DEMANDING MATURATION PROCESS IN TERMS OF TEMPERATURE AND HUMIDITY.

STEPS OF PRODUCTION
Seeding (lactic acids and rennet), curdling, brewing, manual moulding with a ladle, slow occasional draining for 24 hours, salting with dry salt, drying for 10 days between 6 and 12ºC. Maturation from 4 to 8 weeks in a cellar, between 4 and 14 ºC, at a humidity level of 80 to 98%. During the aging, the brie de Melun is turned over once per week in order to achieve the consistent flower shape on each face.

CUTTING
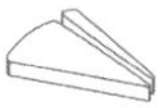
In slices, from the crust to the heart.

BEST TASTING PERIOD
April to September.

SERVING
A slightly chillier temperature is suggested; remove from refrigerator 30 minutes before serving.

STORAGE
Between 4 and 8 ºC in the crisper, in its original packaging or wax paper.

REGION/PROVINCE
Normandy, Aube, Côte-d'Or, Saône-et-Loire.

MILK AND FEEDING
Whole cow's milk. Cows: all breeds. Fodder and pasture grazing, silage.

APPEARANCE
Fine and consistent, very creamy and gooey, fine crust, velvety white; surface mould if more mature.

TASTE & FLAVOUR
Balanced and buttery, lightly salty; taste of mushrooms, undergrowth, notes of fruit and hazelnuts, when more mature.

ACCOMPANIMENTS
Country-style bread, baguette, general bread, fresh or dried fruits, fresh herbs (chives, thyme, etc.).

WINES
Dry, lively whites make for the most suitable pairing: chenin, chardonnay or sauvignon.

AOP/PGI (PROTECTED GEOGRAPHIC INDICATION):
APPROVAL IN PROGRESS/PGI SINCE FEBRUARY 2017

BRILLAT-SAVARIN

FORMERLY KNOWN UNDER THE NAME "EXCELSIOR" OR "GOURMET'S DELIGHT", IT IS HENRI ANDROUET, FOUNDER OF THE FIRST PARISIAN CHEESE FACTORY IN 1909 WHO RENAMED IT IN HONOUR OF THE FAMOUS GASTRONOME AND AUTHOR OF THE *HANDBOOK OF GASTRONOMY*.

THIS TRIPLE CREAM CHEESE, THE "FOIE GRAS OF CHEESE", WITH THE ADDITION OF CREAM INTO THE RAW MILK, ITS SLOW CURDLING AND OCCASIONAL DRAINING MAKE FOR A PARTICULARLY CREAMY PRODUCT THAT MELTS IN THE MOUTH.

IT EXISTS IN TWO VERSIONS, EITHER FRESH OR AGED, AND TWO DIFFERENT SIZE FORMATS (200G OR 500G).

STEPS OF PRODUCTION
Mixing of cream and milk, coagulation by lactic acid and rennet, coagulation, moulding, occasional drying, salting, drying. Maturation of 5 to 8 days for the fresh variety, or 5 to 8 weeks for the aged variety.

CUTTING

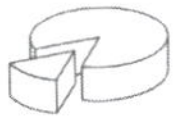

In quarters.

BEST TASTING PERIOD
April to October.

SERVING
Room temperature; take it out 2 hours before tasting.

STORAGE
8 ° C in the crisper of the refrigerator, in its original packaging.

REGION
Normandie, Calvados, Manche, Orne, Eure

MILK AND FEEDING
Raw cow's milk. Cows: Norman cows. Fodder and pasture grazing (6 months minimum).

APPEARANCE
Chalky core; smooth and soft throughout, from ivory to yellow in colour.

TASTE AND FLAVOUR
Milky and sweet when less ripened; strong and fruity at full maturity.

ACCOMPANIMENTS
Country-style bread, whole grain bread, gingerbread, dried fruits, fresh grapes, red berry jam or frozen berries or cider, honey.

WINES
Don't hold back! Cider is a camembert's best friend. If you are allergic to cider, you can go for a low tannin red wine : chinon, touraine, Alsatian pinot noir...

AOC/AOP : 1983/1996

CAMEMBERT

THE MOST EMBLEMATIC CHEESE OF FRENCH CUISINE, IT CAME INTO THE PUBLIC DOMAIN IN 1926 AND HAS SINCE BEEN PRODUCED IN ALL OF FRANCE AND EVEN BEYOND OUR BORDERS. UNDER THIS GENERIC NAME, ONE MAY FIND A WIDE VARIETY OF PRODUCTS THAT HAVE VERY LITTLE TO DO WITH THE CHEESE OF NORMAN ORIGIN, BORN IN 1791 FROM THE GENIUS OF MARIE HAREL.

PROTECTED SINCE 1983 BY AN AOC, THIS CERTIFICATION THAT GUARANTEES A PRODUCTION ON A DESIGNATED APPELLATION ZONE AND THE RESPECT OF TRADITIONAL CHEESE MAKING PRACTICES.

THE TRUE CAMEMBERT FROM NORMANDY IS 10 TO 11 CM IN DIAMETER, WITH A WHITE, SMOOTH AND LIGHTLY RUFFLED CRUST, STREAKED AND LINED WITH RED. IT IS SOFT TO THE TOUCH.

IT OWES ITS POPULARITY TO THE ICONIC WOODEN BOX IN WHICH IT HAS BEEN SOLD SINCE 1890 AND WHICH, ALLOWING FOR EASIER TRANSPORT, FACILITATED ITS DISTRIBUTION OVER A WIDE TERRITORY.

STEPS OF PRODUCTION
Skimming or natural creaming of the milk, aging of the milk, coagulation by added rennet, light slicing of the curd, moulding with automatic or manual ladle, slow intermittent draining, light pressing, salting with dry salt, 13 days minimum maturation in a hâloir (dryer) between 10 and 18 °C. 30 to 35 days of maturation for a camembert through and through.

CUTTING

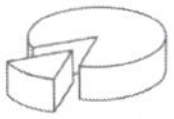

In quarters.

BEST TASTING PERIOD
April to August.

SERVING
Slightly cooler than room temperature, 18 °C. Remove 1 hour before serving if it was kept in the refrigerator.

STORAGE
Avoid refrigeration, better to store it in a dark, chilly room (between 8 and 9 °C). To store it or age it during hot weather, wrap it up inside several sheets of newspaper and place it in its box inside the crisper.

REGION
Aube, Yonne.

MILK AND FEEDING
Raw cow's milk, whole. All cows in the designation area. Fodder taken 85% from the designation area; pasture grazing for 5 months.

APPEARANCE
White, soft and melts in the mouth. Somewhat chalky core for the less mature varieties.

TASTE AND FLAVOUR
Slightly salty, fruity notes of hazelnut, fresh mushrooms, and cream; slightly acidic.

ACCOMPANIMENTS
Crispy baguette, breads without a too marked flavour; fresh herbs (tarragon, chives, etc.), fresh fruit.

WINES
Lively Burgundy whites (chardonnay). For a red: go for something with blended tannins: a côtes-du-jura in a poulsard or trousseau would be nice.

AOC/AOP : 1970/1996

CHAOURCE

THIS LIGHTLY ACIDIC CHEESE WITH A LACTIC CURD AND FRESH TASTE IS SOLD IN TWO FORMS: 11 TO 15 CM, AND 8 TO 9 CM FOR THE LITTLE ONES. THE LONG CURDLING OF THE MILK AND SLOW DRAINING, DONE WITHOUT FLIPPING, GIVES THIS CHEESE A CREAMY AND SOFT TEXTURE. SUMMER AND AUTUMN BRING OUT ITS BEST FLAVOURS.

THE RICH GRASSES OF THE CLAY SOIL, IN WHICH THE COWS GRAZE FOR AT LEAST 5 MONTHS, GIVE THIS CHEESE A SWEET NUTTY FLAVOUR.

ITS PRODUCTION WAS DEVELOPED DURING THE MIDDLE AGES, IN NUMEROUS REGIONAL ABBEYS. SUBSEQUENTLY PRODUCED ON FARMS FOR A FAMILY-STYLE CONSUMPTION, IT ROSE IN POPULARITY THANKS TO THE 'COSSONIERS' (WANDERING SALESMEN) WHO, DURING THE 19TH CENTURY, COLLECTED THE SURPLUS CHEESE FROM FARMS AND DISTRIBUTED THEM IN REGIONAL MARKETS AS WELL AS THOSE IN MAJOR CITIES LIKE LYON AND PARIS.

FORMERLY CALLED «TROYES», ÉMILE ZOLA MENTIONS CHAOURCE IN HIS DESCRIPTION OF THE HALLES OF PARIS (IN THE BELLY OF PARIS).

STEPS OF PRODUCTION
Aging of milk, coagulation with lactic acids, moulding with ladle, slow occasional draining, salting of the surface with dry salt, drying on rye straw or stainless steel grill, salting: 14 days of maturation.

CUTTING

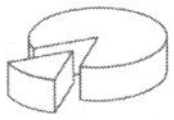

In quarters.

BEST TASTING PERIOD
June to October.

SERVING
Room temperature; allow to sit at room temperature for 1 hour before tasting.

STORAGE
Around 8 °C, in the crisper, in its original packaging, wax paper or parchment paper.

REGION
Île-de-France and more specifically Seine-et-Marne

MILK AND FEEDING
Cow.
Cows: all breeds.
Fodder and pasture grazing.

APPEARANCE
Pale yellow, smooth, creamy and gooey, runny with maturity, fine crust quilted in white fuzz, small orange spots when very ripe.

TASTE AND FLAVOUR
Flavours of cream and mushrooms; typical brie taste with a strong earthy odour.

ACCOMPANIMENTS
Country-style bread, bread with dried fruits (raisins, apricots, figs).

WINES
A supple red wine from the Loire region would work perfectly: bourgueil, chinon and anjou village (cabernet franc), but why not go with a beaujolais (gamay).

AOC/AOP: NONE

COULOMMIERS

THE COULOMMIERS BELONGS TO THE BRIE FAMILY. DENSER THAN A CLASSIC BRIE, IT IS ALSO RECOGNIZABLE BY ITS SLIGHTLY SMALLER DIAMETER. FORMERLY KNOWN AS «LITTLE BRIE» OR «SMALL MOULD BRIE», IT WAS ORIGINALLY CREATED TO FACILITATE TRANSPORTATION - LARGER CHEESES BEING EASILY BROKEN IN THE PROCESS.

ITS RISE IN POPULARITY COMES FROM ITS FIRST PRESENTATION AT THE 1878 WORLD'S FAIR. MADE IN SEINE-ET-MARNE, IT DOES NOT HAVE AN AOP DESIGNATION. IN ORDER TO APPRECIATE THE FULL RICHNESS OF THIS CHEESE, IT IS RECOMMENDED TO BUY IT FARM-PRODUCED, A GUARANTEE OF QUALITY AND OF A RESPECT FOR PRODUCTION TRADITIONS.

STEPS OF PRODUCTION
Partial skimming, curdling (rennet), slicing of the curd then manual moulding with a brie shovel for farm-produced cheeses, draining, individual salting with dry salt; maturation from 3 to 8 weeks.

CUTTING
In slices, from the centre out to the crust.

BEST TASTING PERIOD
October to May; ideally from April to August.

SERVING
A slightly chillier temperature is suggested; remove from refrigerator 30 minutes before serving.

STORAGE
Between 4 and 8 °C in the crisper, in its original packaging or wax paper.

REGION
Auvergne,
Puy-de-Dôme.

MILK AND FEEDING
Milk: Raw or pasteurized cow's milk.
Cows: all breeds.
Feeding: all types.

APPEARANCE
White to cream, crumbly and brittle to smooth according to ripening, dotted with small pieces of herbs and pepper; thin, mould crust.

TASTE AND FLAVOUR
Fresh, lactic, pungent and garlic taste, long in the mouth.

ACCOMPANIMENTS
Green salad, walnut, or baked for a few minutes on toast and served as an appetizer.

WINES
A red with little tannins would go well: cabernet franc, cabernet-sauvignon, malbec.

AOC/AOP: NONE

GAPERON

THIS SMALL, SOFT-DOUGH CHEESE WITH A DOME-SHAPED MOULD RIND IS FLAVOURED WITH GARLIC AND PEPPER. THE PLAIN OF LIMAGNE, OF WHICH IT ORIGINATES, IS ALSO THE CAPITAL OF GARLIC IN AUVERGNE. ONCE PRODUCED WITH THE RESIDUAL WHEY FROM BUTTER MAKING, IT OWES ITS NAME TO «GASPE» WHICH MEANS BUTTERMILK IN THE LOCAL DIALECT. IT IS NOW PRODUCED FROM SOUR MILK, SOMETIMES STILL SPRINKLED WITH BUTTERMILK IN RECOGNITION OF TRADITION.

THERE IS A «GAPERON STRING» WRAPPED IN RAFFIA THAT REQUIRES A LONGER REFINEMENT.

THE GAPERONS WERE ONCE HUNG ON FARM TRUSSES, THE BUTTER BEING A SIGN OF PROSPERITY, THEIR NUMBER WAS CALCULATED INTO A BRIDE'S DOWRY.

STEPS OF PRODUCTION
Lactic coagulation, first moulding and draining with a rag, salting and flavouring (pepper and crushed garlic), second casting, pressing and draining. Ripening from 3 to 4 weeks, in wet cellars on rye straw. The «gaperon string» is renneted and aged for 2 months.

CUTTING

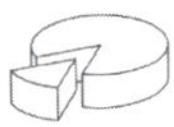

In quarters.

BEST TASTING PERIOD
May to October.

SERVING
Cooler than room temperature if not aged. At room temperature for a «gaperon string», remove from refrigerator 30 minutes before tasting.

STORAGE
Around 8 °C, in the refrigerator's crisper, packaged in its original paper.

REGION
Pays de Bray, Oise, Seine-Maritime.

MILK AND FEEDING
Cow's milk, raw or pasteurized. Cows: Norman cattle at 60% of the herd. Fodder of 80% of production area, pasture grazing for 6 months.

APPEARANCE
Firm, creamy and smooth; flowery, fine and smooth rind.

TASTE AND FLAVOUR
Lightly salty, milky - delicate, refined flavour.

ACCOMPANIMENTS
Sweet breads, baguette, pain brié (Norman specialty), basil, apple, pear, fig, pine nuts.

WINES
Go for a regional pairing : a cider would do well. Choose a rather fruity red wine in case cider isn't your thing. If the neufchâtel is ripe, a red with more tannin is recommended.

AOC/AOP : 1969/1996

NEUFCHÂTEL

NEUFCHÂTEL COMES IN A VARIETY OF FORMS: BRIQUETTES, SQUARES, CYLINDERS OR EVEN IN THE SHAPE OF A HEART. WHEN IN A RIPE STAGE, ITS CORE TAKES ON A GOLDEN YELLOW COLOUR.

THE CLAY SOIL OF THE BRAY REGION AND COOL, RAINY CLIMATE MAKE FOR RICH GRASSES THAT GIVE THE MILK ITS AROMATIC PROPERTIES. THE CLIMATE CONDITIONS ARE CONDUCIVE TO THE BACTERIA PENICILLIUM, WHICH GIVES THE RIND ITS PARTICULAR FELT TEXTURE.

THIS WOULD REMAIN A SECRET UNTIL THE 17TH CENTURY, WHEN THE DRYING OUT OF WETLANDS WILL ALLOW FOR THE DEVELOPMENTS OF PRAIRIES AND THUS AN INCREASE IN MILK PRODUCTION IN THE AREA.

IT COMES INTO FAME THANKS TO NAPOLÉON BONAPARTE DURING THE 19TH CENTURY.

ACCORDING TO LEGEND, IT OWES ITS HEART SHAPE TO THE YOUNG GIRLS IN LOVE WHO, DURING THE HUNDRED YEARS' WAR, WOULD DECLARE THEIR FEELINGS BY GIVING HEART-SHAPED CHEESES TO ENGLISH SOLDIERS.

STEPS OF PRODUCTION
Coagulation through added lactic ferments, slow draining in a bag or canvas, no pressing, then slow draining, mixing then moulding, salting with dry salt, seeding with Penicillim candidum; ripening between 10 and 14 °C for 10 days minimum.

CUTTING

In quarters, from the centre out (for the heart-shape, square or briquette).

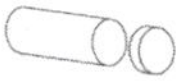

In round slices (when a cylinder).

BEST TASTING PERIOD
May to August.

SERVING
Room temperature, remove from the refrigerator 1 hour before tasting.

STORAGE
In the crisper, in original packaging.

REGION
Auvergne, Rhône-Alpes, Isère, Drôme.

MILK AND FEEDING
Raw cow's milk, whole. Cows: any breed.

APPEARANCE
Very creamy; from firm to runny according to maturity; yellow to bluish grey rind.

TASTEAND FLAVOUR
Lightly salty with nutty flavours; milky when young, strong and long in the mouth when mature.

ACCOMPANIMENTS
Vienna bread, bread with dried fruits, olive bread.

WINES
The saint-félicien marries well with a Rhône valley red (grenache, syrah, mourvèdre, cinsault) : vacqueyras, saint-joseph, côtes-du-rhône, gigondas...

AOC/AOP: NONE

SAINT-FÉLICIEN

THIS SEMI-AGED CHEESE, OF A LACTIC CURD, AND DOUBLE CREAM, HAS A PRODUCTION PROCESS SIMILAR TO THAT OF THE SAINT-MARCELLIN WITH WHICH IT SHARES A SOIL TYPE. IT IS DISTINGUISHED BY ITS SOMEWHAT MORE IMPOSING SIZE (150 G RATHER THAN 80 G), A SIMPLER MATURATION AND THE ADDITION OF CREAM, WHICH GIVES IT ITS CHARACTERISTIC CREAMINESS.

MADE ORIGINALLY FROM GOAT MILK FROM THE NORTH OF THE ARDÈCHE, IN THE VILLAGE OF SAINT-FÉLICIEN, IT IS MANUFACTURED TODAY IN THE DRÔME AND IN ISÈRE; AND COW'S MILK HAS REPLACED THE TRADITIONAL GOAT MILK. EVEN THOUGH THE PRODUCERS IN THE ARDÈCHE CAN NO LONGER LAY CLAIM TO THIS APPELLATION, ONE CAN STILL FIND THE ORIGINAL UNDER THE NAME «SOFT CURD OF SAINT-FÉLICIEN».

STEPS OF PRODUCTION
Curdling then addition of cream, aging then coagulation with the addition of lactic ferments and rennet, moulding, draining and salting with dry salt. Maturation for 10 to 28 days.

CUTTING

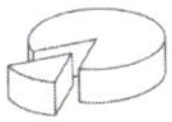

In quarters.

BEST TASTING PERIOD
April to September.

SERVING
Room temperature, remove from the refrigerator a half an hour before tasting.

STORAGE
Between 4 and 8 °C, in the crisper, in original box or packaging.

REGION
Rhône-Alpes, Isère, Drôme, some communes of Savoie.

MILK AND FEEDING
Cow's milk, whole. Cows: all breeds. Fodder, pasture grazing for 180 days per year minimum.

APPEARANCE
Creamy, gooey to runny for the sweet variety, firm for the dry; white, beige or blue-grey rind.

TASTE AND FLAVOUR
Pronounced milky flavours, light saltiness, honey-like fruity taste.

ACCOMPANIMENTS
Vienna bread, dried fruit, frozen fruits, honey, aromatic herbs (thyme, chives, etc.).

WINES
A light red wine, without too much tannin: gamay cépage. A white wine - saint-péray (marsanne, roussanne) - will work perfectly.

PGI (PROTECTED GEOGRAPHIC INDICATION): 2013

SAINT-MARCELLIN

A SMALL CREAMY COW'S MILK CHEESE, IT BOASTS A EUROPEAN CERTIFICATION, THE PGI SINCE 2013, STATING THAT AT LEAST A PART OF ITS PRODUCTION IS ATTACHED TO ITS REGION OF ORIGIN.

IT IS FOUND IN TWO FORMS: DRY, BOASTING A LONGER LASTING CONSERVATION; SWEET, WITH A CREAMIER TEXTURE AND MORE PRONOUNCED FLAVOUR.

ORIGINALLY PRODUCED EXCLUSIVELY IN ISÈRE, FROM A MIXTURE OF COW AND GOAT MILK, IT'S FROM THE MARKET OF THE EPONYMOUS VILLAGE IN THE 15TH CENTURY THAT IT ACQUIRES ITS NAME.

IT IS USUALLY PACKAGED IN A TERRACOTTA RAMEKIN THAT PROTECTS IT FROM DRYING OUT. THE PGI CERTIFICATION BEARING THE COLOURS OF THE EUROPEAN FLAG GUARANTEES THE RELIABILITY AND QUALITY OF THE PRODUCT.

STEPS OF PRODUCTION
Aging and coagulation of milk with lactic ferments and rennet, moulding, draining and salting with dry salt. Aging through drying in an hâloir between 7 and 14 °C for at least 6 weeks.

CUTTING

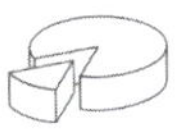

In quarters.

BEST TASTING PERIOD
April to September.

SERVING
Room temperature, remove from the refrigerator 1 hour before tasting.

STORAGE
Around 8 °C, in the crisper, wrapped in original paper or in parchment paper.

SOFT CHEESE WITH WASHED RIND

REGION
Burgundy.

MILK AND FEEDING
Cow's milk. Cows: brown, French Montbéliarde or Simmental. Fodder from 85% of the geographic area and pasture grazing for at least 15 June.

APPEARANCE
Light beige, soft, supple and creamy.

TASTE AND FLAVOUR
Sweet and milky to pungent and spicy, depending on the length of maturation. When ripe, it has a strong taste.

ACCOMPANIMENTS
Sourdough bread, sesame seed bread, or nut or raison bread; pears, figs, grapes.

WINES
Don't wander off too far - Burgundy has what you're looking for. White (chardonnay): meursault, chablis or red (pinot noir): gevrey-chambertin.

AOC/AOP : 1991/1996

ÉPOISSES

CROWNED AS THE KING OF CHEESES IN 1925 BY BRILLAT-SAVARIN, THE FAMOUS AUTHOR OF THE *HANDBOOK OF TASTE*, IT WAS BORN IN THE 17TH CENTURY, IN A COMMUNITY OF CISTERCIAN MONKS ESTABLISHED AT ÉPOISSES, A SMALL VILLAGE ON THE CÔTE-D'OR. IT WAS INSPIRED BY THE MAROILLES.

ITS TRADE SECRETS WERE LATER PASSED ON TO THE FARMERS IN THE AREA WHO CONTRIBUTED TO ITS DEVELOPMENT.

ÉPOISSES IS A LACTIC CURD CHEESE, MEANING THAT THE MILK IS SLOWLY COAGULATED BY ADDING ENZYMES AND NOT RENNET. THIS RIND-WASHED CHEESE OWES ITS ORANGE COLOUR TO THE 'RED ENZYME', A BACTERIA IN THE WASHING SOLUTION.

THE FLORA IN THE CALCIUM AND CLAY SOILS OF THE REGION (SO-CALLED LIASIQUE) PRODUCES A MILK RICHER IN MINERALS, AIDING IN THE FERMENTATION PROCESS AND GIVING THE ÉPOISSES ITS INIMITABLE CREAMINESS. THE ADDITION OF THE BURGUNDY MARC DURING THE MATURATION PERIOD GIVES IT ITS UNIQUE TASTE.

STEPS OF PRODUCTION
Lactic clotting with added lactic enzymes, moulded with a ladle, occasional draining without pressing and then salting. During the maturation of 4 to 8 weeks, the cheese is washed several times with a solution with gradually increased amounts of Burgundy marc.

CUTTING

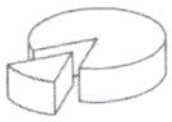

In quarters.

BEST TASTING PERIOD
May to October.

SERVING
Room temperature; allow to sit at room temperature for 1 hour before tasting.

STORAGE
In the crisper, in original packaging.

REGION
Champagne-Ardenne, Burgundy

MILK AND FEEDING
Cow's milk. Cows: at least 50% Montbéliarde, brown or Simmental. Fodder from 80% of the designation area, pasture grazing for 6 months.

APPEARANCE
White and creamy, granular texture when young, gooey and creamy when ripened, the core is sometimes chalky.

TASTE AND FLAVOUR
Slightly tart, flavours of peat and yeast long-lasting in the mouth.

ACCOMPANIMENTS
Country-style bread, nuts, apples, quince paste, cumin.

WINES
A pinot noir or chardonnay is preferable. Burgundies go really well with the langres: saint-aubin (white), volnay (red) for example.

AOC/AOP : 1991/1996

LANGRES

COUSIN AND GEOGRAPHIC NEIGHBOUR TO THE ÉPOISSES, IT OWES ITS NAME TO THE CITY OF LANGRES IN CHAMPAGNE, AROUND WHICH IT IS PRODUCED.

CAST IN A TERRACOTTA MOULD CALLED A «FROMOTTE» AND THEN AGED IN STONEWARE POTS, THE LANGRES IS CHARACTERIZED BY A PEAK INSIDE THE ITS WELL-SHAPED DEPRESSION, WHICH IS ACHIEVED BY A NATURAL AGING DONE WITHOUT FLIPPING. THE IMPORTANCE OF THIS HOLLOW IS AS AN INDICATOR OF THE DEGREE OF MATURITY. ONE CAN POUR A BIT OF BURGUNDY OR CHAMPAGNE MARC INTO THE DENT FOR A MORE TYPICAL TASTING EXPERIENCE.

IT OWES ITS ORANGE COLOUR TO THE PRESENCE OF ACHIOTE (PLANT IMPORTED IN THE 17TH CENTURY FROM SOUTH AMERICA) IN THE WASHING SOLUTION.

IT IS FOUND FOR SALE IN DIFFERENT VARIETIES: SMALL (150 TO 250 G, 15 DAYS OF AGING); MEDIUM (250 TO 380 G, 18 DAYS) AND LARGE (800 G TO 1.3 KG, 21 DAYS).

STEPS OF PRODUCTION
Rennet added to milk, slow coagulation, then cutting and moulding of the curd, occasional drying in the mould cast for 15 hours at least, release from the mould, salting and aging from 15 to 21 days.

CUTTING

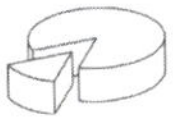

In quarters.

BEST TASTING PERIOD
May to August.

SERVING
Room temperature; allow to sit at room temperature for a half an hour before tasting.

STORAGE
In an airtight container in the crisper of the refrigerator.

REGION
Normandy (pays d'Auge).

MILK AND FEEDING
Cow's milk. Cows: Norman breeds. Fodder and pasture grazing (6 months minimum).

APPEARANCE
Soft, melting, dark yellow in colour, slightly airy.

TASTE AND FLAVOUR
Salty taste, strong and persistent flavours of flowers, barn, smoky notes that evoke cured meats.

ACCOMPANIMENTS
Cumin, cumin bread, rye bread, sourdough, apples.

WINES
A sweet white wine from the Loire region (chenin) with a light residual sugar content pairs well with the livarot: a montlouis or a coteaux-du-layon.

AOC/AOP : 1975/1996

LIVAROT

ITS SHINY AND VISCOUS CRUST HOUSES A GOOEY CENTRE WITH STRONG FLAVOURS.

ONE OF THE OLDEST NORMAN CHEESES, IT DRAWS ITS STRONG FLAVOURS FROM THE RICH PRAIRIES OF THE AUGE REGION AND THE EXCEPTIONAL LACTATION OF THE NORMAN COWS.

RICH AND VERY FRAGRANT, IT WAS CONSIDERED IN THE 19TH CENTURY AS 'THE MEAT OF THE POOR'.

STILL MARKETED WRAPPED IN SEDGE, A KIND OF STRIP OF DRIED REED, THAT KEEPS IT DURING ITS RIPENING, THIS «ADORNMENT», THAT LOOK LIKE AN OFFICER'S STRIPES, GAVE IT ITS NICKNAME COLONEL.

IT COMES IN FOUR VARIETIES, FROM 9 TO 20 CM IN DIAMETER: LITTLE LIVAROT, 3/4 LIVAROT, LIVAROT, AND LARGE LIVAROT.

STEPS OF PRODUCTION
Maturation of milk, coagulation (rennet), cutting of the curd, moulding and draining, salting with salt or in brine; aging from 21 to 35 days depending on variety: drying in an hâloir, washing and brushing of the rind, wrapping of the cheese in natural straps (sedge); additional ripening in cellar if necessary.

CUTTING

In quarters.

BEST TASTING PERIOD
May to September.

SERVING
Room temperature, remove from the refrigerator 1 hour before tasting.

STORAGE
In the crisper of the refrigerator, in its box or paper, or wrapped in a cloth.

REGION
Nord-Pas-de-Calais, Thierache, Nord, Aisne.

MILK AND FEEDING
Cow's milk.
Cows: all breeds.
Fodder and pasture grazing for at least 170 days.

APPEARANCE
Soft and creamy, white or cream in colour with small openings.

TASTEAND FLAVOUR
Milky taste, slightly salty, flavours of curdled milk, hazelnuts with hints of onion, acidity and light bitterness.

ACCOMPANIMENTS
Country-style bread, nut or cumin bread, endives, nuts, cured ham.

WINES
Go more for an abbey beer rather than wine. If you can't stand beer, go for a white wine with residual sugar: Alsatian gewurztraminer, bonnezeaux (chenin).

AOC/AOP : 1976/1996

MAROILLES

A SQUARE-SHAPED CHEESE, ITS ORANGE-RED CRUST REVEALS A SOFT AND CREAMY CENTRE WITH A FULL-BODIED FLAVOUR.

CREATED IN 930 IN THE ABBEY OF MAROILLES, IT COMES ORIGINALLY FROM THE THIÉRACHE, IN THE NORTHEAST OF FRANCE.

THE MAROILLES IS A CHEESE WITH A TIGHT CURD, AGED FROM 3 TO 5 WEEKS, BRUSHED AND WASHED IN SALT WATER. THE USE OF THE RED BACTERIA (BREVIBACTERIUM LINENS) IN THE WASHING SOLUTION GIVES THE CRUST THIS COLOUR, GOING FROM ORANGE TO OCHRE, AS WELL AS ITS STRONG AND PERSISTENT ODOUR.

IT COUNTS AMONG ITS FANS SUCH ILLUSTRIOUS PERSONALITIES FROM FRENCH HISTORY AS SAINT LOUIS, PHILIPPE AUGUSTE, CHARLES QUINT, CHARLES VI, FRANÇOIS THE IST, FÉNELON, TURENNE.

STEPS OF PRODUCTION
Acidification of milk then coagulation (rennet), slicing of curds and partial draining, draining in moulds, then into the cellar (more than 16 °C) and flipping, then it's taken from the mould, salted with dry salt or in brine, drying and acculturation for 48 hours in an hâloir. Ripening from 21 to 35 days minimum between 9 and 16 °C, the cheeses are then brushed and washed.

CUTTING

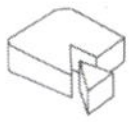

In triangular units.

BEST TASTING PERIOD
May to August.

SERVING
Room temperature, remove from the refrigerator 1 hour before tasting.

STORAGE
In the crisper, in original packaging and once opened, in an airtight box.

REGION
Haut-Doubs.

MILK AND FEEDING
Raw goat's milk, whole. Cows: Montbéliarde or Simmental. Prairie forages in the designation area, pasture grazing.

APPEARANCE
From creamy to very runny, white to ivory in colour, pleated, pale yellow rind.

TASTE AND FLAVOUR
Slightly salty taste, woody, animal and milky flavours.

ACCOMPANIMENTS
Brioche, rye bread, smoked charcuterie (smoked ham, Morteau sausage).

WINES
White wines from the Jura (with a savagnin cépage) are its friends: arbois, dôtes-du-jura, château-chalon, l'étoile.

AOC/AOP : 1981/1996

MONT D'OR

THIS HIGH-ALTITUDE CHEESE, GENERALLY SERVED VERY RUNNY, IS SEASONAL - ONLY SOLD FROM SEPTEMBER TO MAY AND PRODUCED FROM THE 15TH OF AUGUST TO THE 15TH OF MARCH.

IT TAKES ITS NAME FROM THE HIGHEST POINT OF THE HAUT-DOUBS. HISTORICALLY, THESE ARE THE CLIMATIC CONDITIONS THAT HAVE LED FARMERS TO PRODUCE A SMALLER CHEESE, MORE SUITED TO LOW MILK PRODUCTION IN THE HARSH WINTERS OF THE HIGH MOUNTAINS.

THE MONT D'OR OR VACHERIN OF HAUT-DOUBS IS A VERY RUNNY CHEESE, AGED ON SPRUCE PLANKS, A WOOD THAT IS ALSO USED FOR THE MANUFACTURING OF THE STRAPS AND BOXES IN WHICH IT IS PRESENTED.

WHEN IT IS VERY AGED, IT IS EATEN WITH A SPOON.

DELICIOUS WHEN HOT, TRY IT MELTED WITH POTATOES AND CHARCUTERIE, BY PLACING THE BOX, WRAPPED IN ALUMINIUM FOIL, FOR A HALF AN HOUR IN THE OVEN!

STEPS OF PRODUCTION
Coagulation of milk (rennet), pressing in cylindrical moulds. After release from moulds, the curd is wrapped into a strap of spruce. Aging for 21 days minimum: in a cellar on spruce planks, the cheese is flipped and rubbed with salt water, the ripening takes place in a spruce box after the 12th days.

CUTTING

Remove the rind carefully with the tip of a knife then serve with a spoon; in quarters if served firm.

BEST TASTING PERIOD
September to May.

SERVING
Room temperature, remove from the refrigerator 1 hour before tasting, or melted in the oven.

STORAGE
Less than 12 °C, in a cool room or in the crisper in its original packaging.

REGION
Alsace-Lorraine

MILK AND FEEDING
Cow's milk raw or pasteurized. Cows: Holstein, Montbéliarde, Vosges. Forage and pasture grazing.

APPEARANCE
Both firm and supple, creamy; smooth rind, yellow-orange to red-orange in colour.

TASTE AND FLAVOUR
Fine, strong and spicy, soft mouth feel.

ACCOMPANIMENTS
Whole grain bread, caraway or bread with caraway, cumin or cumin bread, nuts or nut bread; serve with mustard when it is young.

WINES
Alsatian whites are the munster's friend: gewurztraminer, pinot gris, pinot blanc, you'd be hard-pressed to find a better pairing.

AOC/AOP : 1969/1996

MUNSTER

THIS CHEESE WITH A SOFT CORE AND PARTICULARLY FRAGRANT, WASHED RIND, IS PRODUCED IN ALSACE AND LORRAINE, MORE PRECISELY IN THE VOSGES FOR THE MUNSTER-GÉROMÉ, THE NAME OF THE TOWN OF GÉRARDMER, AS PRONOUNCED IN THE LOCAL DIALECT, WHERE IT IS HISTORICALLY SOLD. IT IS ALSO FOUND IN A SMALLER VERSION, «LITTLE MUNSTER.»

THE WORD «MUNSTER» DERIVES FROM THE LATIN *MONASTERIUM*, WHICH INDICATES ITS MONASTIC ORIGIN.

ITS TYPICALLY YELLOW-ORANGE COLOUR IS A RESULT OF THE BACTERIA AND YEASTS FOUND IN THE FLORA UNIQUE TO THE CELLARS OF THE REGION WHERE IT IS AGED. IT IS THE BACTERIA *BREVIBACTERIUM LINENS* «RED FERMENT» THAT GIVES THE MUNSTER ITS CHARACTERISTIC ORANGE COLOUR.

IT IS IMPORTANT TO NOTE THAT ONLY THE CHEESES PRODUCED WITH MILK MADE ON-SITE ARE ALLOWED TO CARRY THE DISTINCTION OF FARM-PRODUCED CHEESE.

STEPS OF PRODUCTION
Fine slicing of the curd, moulding, table top draining with flipping, release from mould, salting and 'halage' (drying). Ripening between 11 and 15 °C for at least 14 days for the little munster, 21 for the munster and munster-géromé. Flipping and washing every two days during the ripening period.

CUTTING

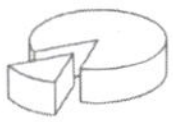

In quarters.

BEST TASTING PERIOD
May to October.

SERVING
At room temperature.

STORAGE
Avoid wrapping it, in Alsace it is preserved in a chilly place held between two plates.

REGION
Normandie,
Calvados, Manche,
Orne, Eure.

MILK AND FEEDING
Cow's milk.
Cows: Norman cattle for at least 50% of the herd.
Fodder and pasture grazing of at least 6 months.

APPEARANCE
Soft, ivory to pale yellow in colour.

TASTE AND FLAVOUR
Sweet tastes, milky flavours of cream, plants, nuts, and smoky notes.

ACCOMPANIMENTS
Country-style bread, baguette, whole grain bread, fresh or dried figs, hazelnuts.

WINES
And why not an old calvados, instead? Don't forget that a regional pairing is most often the best choice, but if you really want wine, go for a pleasant bordeaux.

AOC/AOP : 1972/1996

PONT-L'ÉVÊQUE

A VERY OLD CHEESE FROM LOWER NORMANDY, WELL LOVED SINCE THE MIDDLE AGES, IT OWES ITS NAME TO THE MARKET OF PONT-L'ÉVÊQUE WHERE IT HAS BEEN SOLD SINCE THE 17TH CENTURY.

FORMERLY KNOWN AS «ANGELOT» (CHERUB), IT IS MENTIONED IN THE ROMAN DE LA ROSE, A FAMOUS POEM FROM THE 13TH CENTURY. IT APPEARS ONCE AGAIN, UNDER THE PEN OF ZOLA IN HIS DESCRIPTION OF THE HALLES OF PARIS IN HIS BOOK THE BELLY OF PARIS.

THE USE OF SQUARE WOODEN MOULDS GIVES IT ITS UNIQUE SHAPE, DIFFERENTIATING IT FROM OTHER CHEESES OF THE REGION.

FLIPPED MULTIPLE TIMES DURING THE DRAINING STAGE, THE CREAMINESS OF ITS CORE IS OBTAINED THANKS TO PAINSTAKING WORK CARRIED OUT AT THIS STAGE OF PRODUCTION. THIS PARTICULARLY SAVOURY CHEESE DEVELOPS A SUBTLE TASTE AND FRUITY, MILKY FLAVOURS.

STEPS OF PRODUCTION
Coagulation (rennet), salting, slicing of the curd, moulding, draining and flipping, aging in an hâloir for 8 to 21 days according to desired form at 6 weeks old. Washes in saltwater during ripening.

CUTTING

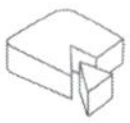

In triangular units.

BEST TASTING PERIOD
May to September

SERVING
At room temperature.

STORAGE
In a cool room, in its original packaging or box.

REGION
Savoie, Haute-Savoie.

MILK AND FEEDING
Raw cow's milk.
Cows: Abondance cattle, Tarine or Montbéliarde.
Grass (pasture) in summer, hay in winter.

APPEARANCE
Creamy and soft, pale yellow in colour; smooth rind, light yellow to ocher.

TASTE AND FLAVOUR
Delicate flavours, subtle hints of hazelnut; creamy, velvety mouth feel.

ACCOMPANIMENTS
Dried fruits (nut bread) and fresh fruits (apricots, pears, figs), cured ham.

WINES
Ideally paired with a white wine from the region, namely Savoie, like chignin-bergeron (chasselas, roussanne, altesse).

AOC/AOP : 1958/1996

REBLOCHON

ITS CHARACTERISTICALLY INTENSE ODOUR CONTRASTS WITH THE CREAMY, SMOOTH TEXTURE OF ITS CORE AND SUBTLE FLAVOURS OF HAZELNUT AND FRESH MILK. IT IS EATEN THROUGHOUT THE YEAR, BUT IT IS IN SUMMER AND AUTUMN WHEN IT REVEALS THE RICH FLAVOURS OF THE PASTURES IN WHICH THE COWS GRAZE FOR 4 TO 5 MONTHS.

INVENTED IN THE 13TH CENTURY, IT OWES ITS NAME TO THE PRACTICE OF THE 'RE-BLOCHE', A SECOND MILKING THAT ALLOWED FARMERS TO KEEP A PORTION OF THE MILK HARVEST FOR THEMSELVES IN FUNCTION OF THE TAXES ('OCIÈGE') THAT THEY WERE REQUIRED TO HANDOVER TO THE LANDOWNERS. THIS SECOND MILKING, SCARCE IN TOTAL OUTPUT, BUT PARTICULARLY RICH IN CREAM WAS FROM THEN ON USED FOR THE MANUFACTURE OF ILLEGAL, SECRET CHEESE. IT HAS HAD AN AOC SINCE 1958.

STEPS OF PRODUCTION
Curdling of milk then moulding. Green sticker for the farm-produced reblochon, red sticker for the dairy farm reblochon. Pressing, salting then pre-aging (one week in dryer) then aging (from 18 to 40 days) in a cellar.

CUTTING

In slices, from centre out.

BEST TASTING PERIOD
July to November.

SERVING
16 °C, cooler than room temperature, take from the refrigerator 1 hour before serving.

STORAGE
Wrapped in original paper, at the bottom of the refrigerator.

REGION
Hauts-de-France, Flandre.

MILK AND FEEDING
Cow's milk.
Cows: any breed.
Forage and pasture grazing.

APPEARANCE
White to ivory in colour, grey, fine and oily rind.

TASTE AND FLAVOUR
Salty taste, distinctive and full-bodied, long in the mouth.

ACCOMPANIMENTS
Country-style bread, nut bread or cumin bread, endives, nuts, cured ham.

WINES
Choose a beer with character, with a high fermentation or an Abbey beer. Otherwise, a nice sweet white: sauternes, côteaux-du-layon, montbazillac.

REGIONAL CERTIFICATION

VIEUX-LILLE

IT COMES WITH A VARIETY OF QUITE EVOCATIVE NAMES: GRIS-DE-LILLE (GRAY LILLE), VIEUX-GRIS-DE-LILLE (OLD GRAY LILLE), MAROILLES GRIS (GRAY MAROILLES), PUANT MACÉRÉ (STEEPED IN STINK), OR PUANT DE LILLE (STINKING LILLE)!

ITS ODOUR IS PARTICULARLY STRONG, EVEN MORE SO THAN THAT OF THE MAROILLES OF WHOM IT IS A CLOSE COUSIN.

THIS SQUARE CHEESE WITH A GREY RIND OWES ITS COLOUR TO A STEEPING IN BRINE THAT GIVES A MARKED SALTY TASTE. THIS EXTENDED BRINING WAS ORIGINALLY MEANT TO ENSURE ITS CONSERVATION DURING THE TRANSPORTATION TO LILLE.

FAVOURITE CHEESE OF MINERS AT THE VERY BEGINNING OF THE 20TH CENTURY, ITS STRONG AND DISTINCTIVE TASTE, AS WELL AS ITS RUNNY TEXTURE, WERE VERY MUCH APPRECIATED AT THE KREMLIN DINING TABLE OF NIKITA KRUSHCHEV.

STEPS OF PRODUCTION
Ccidification of the milk then coagulation (rennet), slicing of the curd and partial draining, draining in the mould, in cellar (more than 16 °C) and flipping. Release from mould, first a dry aging with washing then salting in brine for 3 months. Aging between 5 and 6 months.

CUTTING

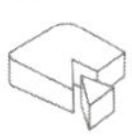

In triangular units.

BEST TASTING PERIOD
November to January.

SERVING
Room temperature, remove from the refrigerator 1 hour before tasting.

STORAGE
In the crisper, in original packaging and once opened, in an airtight box.

UNCOOKED PRESSED CHEESE

REGION
Auvergne.

MILK AND FEEDING
Cow's milk.
Cows: any breed from the designation area.
Fodder, pasture grazing (120 days minimum).

APPEARANCE
Creamy yellow, with white marbling, and soft texture for the young and medium ripe Cantals; dark yellow and crumbly for the more ripe ones.

TASTE AND FLAVOUR
Sweet with milky flavours, taste of pasture for the younger varieties, full-bodied and spicy, for the older types.

ACCOMPANIMENTS
Rye bread, Vienna baguette, dried fruit (raisins, figs, etc.), black cherry jam, chutney.

WINES
Depending on the type of Cantal. For a young, go for a red from Auvergne: gamay. For an medium ripe or ripe: cabernet-sauvignon, cabernet franc, merlot.

AOC/AOP : 1956/1996

CANTAL

MENTIONED 2,000 YEARS AGO IN THE WRITINGS OF PLINY THE ELDER, WRITER AND NATURALIST, IT IS WITHOUT A DOUBT THE OLDEST CHEESE IN THE WORLD.

A TOMME OF CANTAL CAN WEIGH BETWEEN 35 AND 45 KG. THIS IMPOSING SIZE ALLOWED FOR STORAGE OF LARGE QUANTITIES OF THE CHEESE DURING THE HARSH WINTERS OF THE REGION.

IT TAKES 33 HOURS TO PRODUCE ONE TOMME. ITS PARTICULARITY COMES FROM BEING PRESSED TWICE, WHICH GIVES THE CHEESE'S BODY AN EXCEPTIONAL HOLD.

IT IS EATEN IN 3 VERSIONS ACCORDING TO THE LENGTH OF MATURATION: YOUNG, MEDIUM RIPE AND OLD.

STEPS OF PRODUCTION
Coagulation with added rennet, slicing of the curd and brewing, pressing followed by drying through repeated flipping, aging for 10 to 24 hours, the resulting tomme is then ground and salted. Ground manually, it is pressed a second time in order to obtain a firm hold in the body. Maturation in cellar: young Cantal - 30 to 60 days; medium ripe - 90 to 210 days; old Cantal - 240 days minimum.

CUTTING

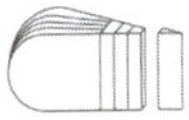

First cut the tip, then into slices running parallel to the crust. From the halfway point of the portion cut, slice vertically, making sure to include the crust.

BEST TASTING PERIOD
June to October.

SERVING
Allow to sit at room temperature for 1 hour before tasting.

STORAGE
In original packaging or in food film, in the crisper.

REGION
Massif de l'Aubrac, Aveyron, Cantal, Lozère.

MILK AND FEEDING
Raw cow's milk, whole. Cows: French Simmental and Aubrac. Fodder from the appellation area and pasture grazing for 150 days minimum.

APPEARANCE
Soft to firm, melting, marbled texture; Brown crust with orange sheen.

TASTE AND FLAVOUR
Medium to intense lactic taste following ripening, fresh hay notes, hazelnuts, long in the mouth. Strong, rustic taste if very refined.

ACCOMPANIMENTS
Baguette, country bread, whole bread, apples, grapes, blueberries, mango.

WINES
A red wine from Aveyron, the marcillac (fer-servadou) would bring out the cheese's flavour well, or if the cheese is rather mature, then a beaujolais (gamay).

AOC/AOP : 1961/1996

LAGUIOLE

IT IS ON THE PLATEAUS OF THE AUBRAC THAT THE VERY ANCIENT FOURME DE LAGUIOLE WAS SLOWLY DEVELOPED. ORIGINALLY CONCEIVED IN A MONASTERY, THE CATHEDRAL OF AUBRAC, ITS PRODUCTION HAS REMAINED SOLELY FARM-BASED. AS A RESULT, THIS TOMME IS ALWAYS DEVELOPED ACCORDING TO TRADITION, IN VERY OLD SHEPHERD'S HUTS CALLED BURONS. THIS CHEESE DRAWS ITS PRAIRIE QUALITY FROM THE ABUNDANT AND VARIED VEGETATION THAT PRODUCES A RICH AND HIGHLY FRAGRANT MILK.

IT IS A MATURE CHEESE THAT IS READY ONLY AFTER SEVERAL MONTHS OF RIPENING.

STEPS OF PRODUCTION
Coagulation (rennet), curd rupture, stirring and casting in vats, pressing, maturing and flipping. Grinding, salting in the mass, casting and pressing. Maturing in cold and humid cellars (6 to 12 ° C), from 4 to 18 months. The cheeses are rubbed and turned throughout the ripening period.

CUTTING

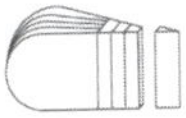

In triangular and rectangular vertical parts, following the shape of the portion.

BEST TASTING PERIOD
September to March.

SERVING
At room temperature.

STORAGE
In a dry and cool place, packed in its original paper.

REGION
Normandie, Meuse.

MILK AND FEEDING
Cow's milk, pasteurized.
Cows: all dairy breeds.
Feeding: all types.

APPEARANCE
Young: Firm and supple;
Aged: crumbly, darker crust.

TASTE AND FLAVOUR
Young: Sweet and fruity, hazelnut flavours; Refined: strong and spicy taste, smoky flavours of caramel and coffee.

ACCOMPANIMENTS
Apple, pear, fresh grapes, dried fruits, hazelnut, endive, mash, saffron, cumin.

WINES
With an older mimolette, strong beer or a strong red wine: médoc, cahors. With a young mimolette, an Abbey beer or a less strong red from Loire.

AOC/AOP: NONE

MIMOLETTE

MIMOLETTE IS ORIGINALLY DUTCH, BUT IN 1675 WHILE FRANCE AND THE NETHERLANDS WERE AT WAR, COLBERT BANNED THE IMPORTATION OF IT AND REQUIRED FLEMISH FARMERS TO DEVELOP A FRENCH ALTERNATIVE.

IT DIFFERS FROM ITS DUTCH COUSIN BY ITS GREY, RUGGED, NON-WAXED CRUST AND SEMI-HARD TO HARD INTERIOR. TO OBTAIN ITS CHARACTERISTIC ORANGE COLOUR, ROCOU (OR ANNATTO) IS ADDED TO THE DOUGH, WHICH IS A CENTRAL AMERICAN PLANT WITH DYEING PROPERTIES.

IT CAN BE EATEN YOUNG, OLD OR VERY OLD - 18 TO 24 MONTHS OF MATURATION ALLOWS FOR THE FULL DEVELOPMENT OF ITS FLAVOURS AND GIVES IT ITS STRONG TASTE AND PARTICULAR BRITTLE TEXTURE, A FAVOURITE AMONG ITS ADMIRERS.

STEPS OF PRODUCTION
Coagulation (rennet) and staining (annatto), slicing of curd, heating, brewing, pressure casting in moulds, salting by brine. Maturing: Young: 3 months; Semi-old: 6 months; Old: 12 months; Extra old: 12 to 24 months. During maturation it is covered in cheese mites, which give the crust its irregularity and allows for moisture to get out - regular brushing. In order to test their quality, the wheels are struck with a mallet, a thud indicates that the product meets standards.

CUTTING

First cut the tip, then into slices running parallel to the crust. From the halfway point of the portion cut, slice vertically, making sure to include the crust. Aged: chip into chunks with the tip of a vegetable peeler.

BEST TASTING PERIOD
April to September.

SERVING
At room temperature, remove it from the refrigerator 1 hour before tasting.

STORAGE
In the refrigerator's crisper, packaged in its original paper or in a rag.

REGION
Franche-Comté, Jura.

MILK AND FEEDING
Cow's milk, raw. Cows: Montbéliarde and French Simmental. Fodder and pasture grazing.

APPEARANCE
Smooth, supple and soft, crossed with a thin grey layer; Moist, thin, smooth crust, powdered pink to orange.

TASTE AND FLAVOUR
Salty and tangy, lactic, vegetable and animal flavours, notes of cream and hazelnuts.

ACCOMPANIMENTS
Country bread, fresh and dried fruit, bacon, cumin.

WINES
The perfect pairing is with a white from Jura: côtes-du-jura, l'étoile (chardonnay, savagnin). You might go ahead and try a red from Jura: pinot noir, poulsard.

AOC/AOP : 2000/2002

MORBIER

PRODUCED IN THE HAUT-JURA MASSIF, IT IS RECOGNIZABLE BY THE FINE GREY LINE THAT CROSSES ITS INTERIOR. THIS CHEESE WAS BORN TWO CENTURIES AGO IN WINTER WHEN MILKING WAS INSUFFICIENT TO PRODUCE WHEELS OF COMTÉ. THE FARMERS THEN MADE THE MORBIER WITH THE TWO MILKINGS OF THE DAY, THE MORNING LAYER WAS PROTECTED WITH ASH, WHICH HAS SINCE BEEN REPLACED BY CHARCOAL.

IT OWES ITS NAME TO THE MARKET OF THE VILLAGE OF MORBIER WHERE THE SHEPHERDS CAME TO SELL IT.

IT IS AN END-OF-MEAL CHEESE, QUITE TYPICAL, WITH A SOFT CORE WITH LACTIC AND VEGETABLE AROMAS.

STEPS OF PRODUCTION
Coagulation, curd cutting, moulding and pressing, when pressing one of the sides is coated with vegetative charcoal. Maturation for 45 days minimum between 7 and 15 ° C during which the cheeses are regularly rubbed with salt water.

CUTTING

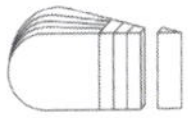

First cut the tip, then slices parallel to the crust. From half-way up the portion, cutting is done in vertical slices including crust.

BEST TASTING PERIOD
April to October.

SERVING
At room temperature. If it has been placed in the refrigerator, take it out 30 minutes before tasting.

STORAGE
In a dry and cool place, packed in its original paper.

REGION
Béarn, Pays basque, Pyrénées-Atlantiques, Hautes-Pyrénées.

MILK AND FEEDING
Raw sheep's milk, whole. Sheep: Basco-Bemanech, Manech. Fodder from the appellation area and pasture grazing for 240 days

APPEARANCE
Firm and tender, creamy, white-ivory to amber. Yellow orange to grey crust.

TASTE AND FLAVOUR
Sweet, lactic, earthy aromas, hazelnut and walnut notes.

ACCOMPANIMENTS
Nut bread, whole grain bread, melon, peach; With a black cherry jam for a traditional tasting or quince paste.

WINES
A dry white with enough body could work: jurançon sec and pacherenc-du-vic-bihl (gros manseng, petit manseng), and for a near perfect pairing go for those same wines, but sweet.

AOC/AOP : 1980/1996

OSSAU-IRATY

THIS PURE SHEEP CHEESE, FROM THE SOUTHWEST, OFFERS A SOFT AND VERY FRAGRANT INTERIOR.

HANDCRAFTED IN THE BÉARN AND THE BASQUE COUNTRY, IT CONTRIBUTES TO SAFEGUARDING THE AGRO-PASTORAL TRADITIONS OF THE REGION. DURING THE SUMMER SEASON, THE MOUNTAIN SHEPHERDS' HUTS, «CUJALAS» IN BÉARN, «CAYOLARS» IN BASQUE, STILL SERVE AS THE PLACE WHERE IT IS PRODUCED.

RESPECTFUL OF THE NATURAL SEASONALITY OF THE SHEEP, THE OSSAU-IRATY CAN ONLY BE PRODUCED IN SEPTEMBER AND OCTOBER.

TRY IT LIKE ONE DOES IN THE BASQUE COUNTRY, PAIRED WITH BLACK CHERRY JAM.

STEPS OF PRODUCTION
Coagulation (rennet), curdling, curd cutting, stirring, casting, pressing with turning, salting or brining, maturing for 3 to 4 months in cool cellars (12 ° C).

CUTTING

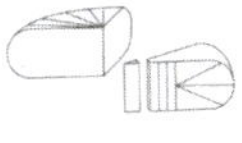

Cut the core into slices parallel to the crust and then, from the half-way point of the slice, trim the heel into a perpendicular slice.

BEST TASTING PERIOD
June to November.

SERVING
At room temperature, remove it from the refrigerator 1 hour before tasting.

STORAGE
In the refrigerator's crisper, packaged in a rag or linen cloth.

REGION
Auvergne

MILK AND FEEDING
Cow's milk.
Cows: all breeds.
Fodder and pasture grazing.

APPEARANCE
Supple and creamy, light yellow; yellow to red crust.

TASTE AND FLAVOUR
Fairly pronounced, lightly salted, milky aromas and hazelnut.

ACCOMPANIMENTS
Bread with sweet flavors like bread with cereal or whole grain bread, mirabelle plum, peach, apricot, walnuts, mushrooms.

WINES
A light and dry red pairs really well with the pavin: gamay, pinot noir.

AOC/AOP: NONE

PAVIN D'AUVERGNE

CLOSE COUSIN OF THE SAINT-NECTAIRE, THE PAVIN IS AN UNCOOKED PRESSED CHEESE WITH A WASHED RIND. PRODUCED ACCORDING TO THE SAME METHODS IN THE MOUNTAINS OF FORETZ IN THE HEART OF AUVERGNE.

IT TAKES ITS NAME FROM A LAKE LOCATED IN THE CRATER OF AN EXTINCT VOLCANO, OFFERING NATURAL CAVES IDEAL FOR ITS REFINEMENT.

ITS CRUST CAN BE ORANGE WHEN THE REFINER ADDS ROUCOU TO THE WASHING SOLUTION.

«ROUCOU» OR «ANNATTO» IS THE FRUIT OF ANNATTO, A CENTRAL AMERICAN SHRUB WHOSE FRUITS ARE USED FOR DYES IN THE RECIPES OF MANY COLOURED RIND CHEESES.

IT IS A CREAMY CHEESE WITH LACTIC FLAVOURS AND A RATHER STRONG TASTE WHICH DELIVERS THE BEST OF ITS AROMAS FROM APRIL TO SEPTEMBER.

STEPS OF PRODUCTION
Coagulation (rennet), slicing of curd, casting, salting, pressing. Maturing for 1 month minimum, in wet cellars with regular washing.

CUTTING

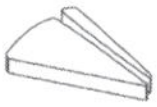

Sliced, from crust to heart.

BEST TASTING PERIOD
April to September.

SERVING
At room temperature, remove it from the refrigerator 1 hour before tasting.

STORAGE
At less than 12 °C, in the refrigerator's crisper, packaged in its original paper.

REGION
Haute-Savoie, Savoie

MILK AND FEEDING
Cow's milk.
Cows: Tarentaise, Abondance, Montbéliarde.
Fodder and pasture grazing.

APPEARANCE
Soft and smooth, white to light yellow, pierced with small holes, orange crust.

TASTE AND FLAVOUR
Lactic, peppery, woody aromas, dry fruit notes.

ACCOMPANIMENTS
Whole grain bread, raw apples and pears, poached or pan-fried, grapes, pineapple, mango, dried apricots, cumin, curry, charcuterie and dried meat.

WINES
Go for a white wine: vin-de-savoie with one of the following cépages: altesse, jacquère, roussanne. But a nice white with a Chardonnay base would work just as well.

PGI (PROTECTED GEOGRAPHIC INDICATION): 2017

RACLETTE DE SAVOIE

IN THE MIDDLE AGES, DURING THE SUMMER, THE SAVOY SHEPHERDS USED TO MELT HALF A WHEEL OF CHEESE IN FRONT OF THE CHIMNEY AND THEN SCRAPE THE MELTED DOUGH WITH A KNIFE TO EAT IT ON A SLICE OF BREAD. IT IS THIS PRACTICE FROM WHICH THIS SAVOY CHEESE TAKES ITS NAME. THE SAVOIE RACLETTE IS EATEN HOT, MELTED WITH CHARCUTERIE AND POTATOES.

THE EXCEPTIONAL RICHNESS OF THE SAVOY ALPS COMBINED WITH THE RESPECT FOR TRADITIONAL MANUFACTURING METHODS MAKE IT A PARTICULARLY CREAMY CHEESE WITH AN ICONIC TASTE, BOTH FRUITY AND WOODY.

STEPS OF PRODUCTION
Coagulation (rennet), slicing of curd, stirring and washing of curds with fresh water, casting and pressing, salting. Maturing in cellars, on wooden planks, between 8 and 13 ° C for 8 weeks minimum.

CUTTING

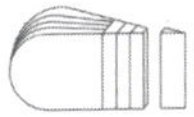

First cut the tip, then slices parallel to the crust. From half-way up the portion, cutting is done in vertical slices including crust.

BEST TASTING PERIOD
November to April.

SERVING
At room temperature, remove it from the refrigerator 1 hour before tasting.

STORAGE
In the refrigerator's crisper, packaged in its original paper or in a rag.

REGION
Auvergne, Puy-de-Dôme, Cantal.

MILK AND FEEDING
Raw cow's milk. Cows: all breeds of cows on the appellation zone. Fodder from the designation area, 140 days pasture grazing minimum.

APPEARANCE
Soft, fine and creamy, cream in colour, pale yellow rind.

TASTE AND FLAVOUR
Taste of fresh milk, of cream, of straw and undergrowth, subtle hints of hazelnut.

ACCOMPANIMENTS
Bread with an airy crumb, whole grain bread.

WINES
Go for a red from the region: saint-pourçain, côtes-d'auvergne (gamay) but you may also turn your attention to a Burgundy pinot noir.

AOC/AOP : 1955/1996

SAINT-NECTAIRE

THE KING OF CHEESES IN THE EYES OF LOUIS XIV, IT OWES ITS NAME AND POPULARITY TO THE MARSHALL HENRI DE SENNECTERRE WHO INTRODUCED IT TO THE SUN KING'S TABLE IN THE 17TH CENTURY.

THE SAINT-NECTAIRE IS PRODUCED IN ONE OF THE SMALLEST ZONES OF PRODUCTION IN EUROPE, ON VOLCANIC LANDS. THE RICH AND FRAGRANT FLORA OF THE PASTURES ON WHICH THE COWS FEED FOR AT LEAST 140 DAYS, COMBINED WITH THE SAVOIR-FAIRE OF REFINERS IN THE SECTOR GIVE IT ITS STRONG, ROBUST TASTE OF CREAM, ITS SUBTLE FLAVOURS OF HAZELNUT AND ITS EXCEPTIONAL CREAMINESS. THE SAINT-NECTAIRE, OF FARM-BASED PRODUCTION, IS EASILY IDENTIFIED THANKS TO ITS OVAL-SHAPED GREEN STICKER. IT RECEIVED AN AOC IN 1955.

STEPS OF PRODUCTION
The curd resulting from the rennet added to the milk is sliced into small chunks then brewed to extract the whey. A first pressing precedes the salting then the casting in mould and the strapping. A second pressing occurs before it's taken from the mould and it is stored in a cold room. The ripening on a bed of rye straw for minimum of 28 days takes place in natural caves.

CUTTING
In slices, from the centre outward.

BEST TASTING PERIOD
April to December.

SERVING
At room temperature, remove it from the refrigerator 1 hour before serving.

STORAGE
Less than 12 °C, in the crisper in its original packaging.

REGION
Auvergne.

MILK AND FEEDING
Raw cow's milk. Cows: Salers and all breeds, (the marking «tradition Salers» guarantees a milk produced by a Salers cow). Pasture grazing.

APPEARANCE
Yellow and even, firm consistency, creamy, crumbly and melting in the mouth

TASTE AND FLAVOUR
Fresh butter when young; herbaceous and fruity to woody and spicy when more ripe.

ACCOMPANIMENTS
Rye bread, Vienna bread, apple, nuts, grapes, red berries.

WINES
Look towards regional reds: côtes-d'auvergne, côteaux-du-quercy (gamay) but you could also wander away a bit, heading towards Burgundy pinot noir.

AOC/AOP : 1961/1996

SALERS

THE SALERS IS PRODUCED IN THE SAME REGION AND ACCORDING TO THE SAME MANUFACTURING PROCESS AS THE CANTAL. ITS SPECIFIC CHARACTER IS DUE TO THE LIMITED PERIOD DURING WHICH IT IS PRODUCED. IT IS ONLY FROM APRIL 15 TO NOVEMBER 15, WHEN THE COWS ARE 'PUT OUT TO FIELD', THAT THE MILK IS HARVESTED AND IMMEDIATELY CURDLED AT THE FARM IN A WOOD CONTAINER CALLED A GERLE.

FROM THE OILY GRASS OF THE MOUNTAINS OF AUVERGNE COMES THIS PARTICULARLY AROMATIC CHEESE WHOSE PALETTE APPEARS ACCORDING TO THE FARMS THAT PRODUCE IT. THE SALERS IS THE ONLY AOP CHEESE THAT IS 100% FARM-PRODUCED.

THE MARKING «TRADITION SALERS» INDICATES THAT THE MILK IS FROM SALERS COWS, WHOSE EXCEPTIONAL PRODUCTION OF MILK IS TYPICAL OF THIS REGION AND OF THE HISTORY OF THIS APPELLATION.

STEPS OF PRODUCTION
Rennet added, curdling then slicing of the curd, brewing, first pressing then draining, acidification through ripening then grinding of the tomme and salting. After a second maturation in salt for 3 hours, the tomme is ground and pressed a second time for 48 hours. Aging from 3 months to 2 years.

CUTTING

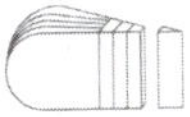

First cut the tip, then into slices running parallel to the crust. From the half way point of the portion cut, slice vertically, making sure to include the crust.

BEST TASTING PERIOD
November to June.

SERVING
Room temperature; allow to sit at room temperature for 1 hour before tasting.

STORAGE
12 °C maximum, in the crisper, in its original paper wrappings.

REGION
Auvergne-Rhône-Alpes, Savoie, Haute-Savoie.

MILK AND FEEDING
Raw cow's milk, skim. Cows: Tarentaise and Abondance (55%), Montbéliarde. Fodder, pasture, 120 days minimum.

APPEARANCE
Soft and melting, ivory to yellow; Thick, grey crust sometimes spotted with yellow, white or red.

TASTE AND FLAVOUR
Sweet, lactic, fruity aromas with a certain acidity.

ACCOMPANIMENTS
Country bread, nut bread, hazelnuts, apples, mango, prunes, endive.

WINES
A white from Savoie: chasselat, roussanne, altesse. For those who cannot go without a red, choose a red pinot noir from Bugey.

AOC/AOP : 2002/2007

TOME DES BAUGES

THE ONLY FRENCH TOMME TO BENEFIT FROM AN AOC, THE TOME DES BAUGES IS CHARACTERIZED BY ITS SMELL OF MUSHROOMS AND MOIST SOIL. ITS SWEET, LACTIC TASTE, AND ITS FRUITY AROMAS DEVELOP DURING RIPENING ON SPRUCE PLANKS. LIKE ALL THE TOMMES OF SAVOY, IT IS A LEAN CHEESE, MADE FROM PARTLY SKIMMED MILK.

PRODUCED EXCLUSIVELY IN THE MASSIF DES BAUGES, IN THE HEART OF THE REGIONAL NATURAL PARK OF THE VOSGES MOUNTAINS, IT WAS RESERVED ONLY FOR DOMESTIC CONSUMPTION UNTIL THE 18TH CENTURY. ITS NAME TOME WITH A SINGLE M COMES FROM THE PATOIS «TOMA» WHICH MEANS CHEESE.

FARM-BASED PRODUCTIONS ARE IDENTIFIED BY A GREEN PLATE AND THE CHEESE MANUFACTURERS, A RED ONE.

STEPS OF PRODUCTION
Maturation, skimming, coagulation (rennet), slicing of the curd, casting, pressing with flipping, dry salt or brine, refining for 5 weeks minimum between 10 and 15 ° C on spruce planks, the cheeses are turned regularly during ripening.

CUTTING

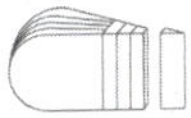

First cut the tip, then slices parallel to the crust.
From half-way up the portion, cutting is done in vertical slices including crust.

BEST TASTING PERIOD
May to August.

SERVING
At room temperature, remove it from the refrigerator 1 hour before tasting.

STORAGE
In the refrigerator's crisper, packaged in its original paper or in a rag.

REGION
Haute-Savoie.

MILK AND FEEDING
Raw or pasteurized cow's milk.
Cows: all breeds.
Fodder and pasture grazing.

APPEARANCE
Double texture: Creamy and chalky, white and soft under crust with a crumbly core; Velvety crust of white and grey.

TASTE AND FLAVOUR
Sweet taste, lactic aromas, fresh, mushrooms, hay, and nuts, delicate acidity.

ACCOMPANIMENTS
Baguette, country bread, cereal, apple, peach, white grape, walnut, almond.

WINES
Light red or fruity white. For reds, pinot noir or gamay: Alsatian pinot noir, bourgogne chitry, touraine, Beaujolais cru. For whites, côteaux-du-languedoc, crépy.

AOC/AOP: NONE

TOMME CRAYEUSE

THIS CHALKY TOMME IS A RECENT CHEESE, WITH AN UNCOOKED, PRESSED DOUGH AND WASHED RIND. ORIGINALLY FROM ANNECY, ALSO PRODUCED IN BRITTANY, ITS PRODUCTION IS SIMILAR TO THE TOMME OF SAVOY. THE IVORY-WHITE COLOUR OF ITS DOUGH ASSOCIATED WITH ITS PLASTERY TEXTURE REMINDS ONE OF THE CHALK FROM WHICH IT TAKES ITS NAME.

THIS CHEESE IS DISTINGUISHED BY A DOUBLE TEXTURE: CREAMY UNDER CRUST AND CRUMBLY AT THE HEART. THIS CHARACTERISTIC IS DUE TO A LONG RIPENING FIRST IN WARM CELLARS, DEVELOPING THE SMOOTHNESS, THEN IN COOL CELLARS THAT SLOWS THE MATURATION LEAVING THE HEART PLASTERY AND TART. THIS RIPENING PROCESS MAKES FOR AN AMAZING CHEESE COMBINING SWEETNESS AND ACIDITY, SMOOTHNESS AND PUNGENTNESS.

STEPS OF PRODUCTION
Seeding, aging, coagulation (rennet), slicing and stirring of the curd, moulding, pressing then draining with flipping, salting with dry salt or in brine. Refining from 1 to 3 months, in warm cellar and then in cool cellars, regular washing of the crust.

CUTTING

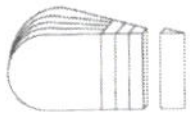

First cut the tip, then slices parallel to the crust. From half-way up the portion, cutting is done in vertical slices including crust.

BEST TASTING PERIOD
August to February.

SERVING
At room temperature, remove it from the refrigerator 1 hour before tasting.

STORAGE
Around 8 °C, in the refrigerator's crisper, packaged in its original paper.

REGION
Auvergne-Rhône-Alpes, Savoie, Haute-Savoie.

MILK AND FEEDING
Raw cow's milk, skim. Cows: Montbéliarde, Tarentaise and 75% Abondance. Fodder and pasture grazing.

APPEARANCE
Half-firm with small openings, white to yellow, grey-white crust.

TASTE AND FLAVOUR
Lightly salted; strong taste, buttery aromas and herbaceous.

ACCOMPANIMENTS
Nuts, hazelnuts, graps, figs, mango, mash, endives.

WINES
A white from Savoie should be first pick: chasselas, roussanne, altesse, but a more Western wine would also be perfect: muscadelle, sémillon.

PGI (PROTECTED GEOGRAPHIC INDICATION): 1996

TOMME DE SAVOIE

UNDER THIS GENERIC TERM THERE ARE MANY CHEESES FROM SAVOY ALL WITH A SIMILAR MANUFACTURING PROCESS. IT IS THE ONLY TOMME TO BE CATEGORISED BASED ON LEVELS OF FAT (FROM 8 TO 30% FAT). THEIR SPECIFICITIES ARE RELATED TO THE KNOW-HOW AND TRICKS OF THE SAVOYARD CHEESES LIKE THE TOMME IN MARC, MATURED SLOWLY IN GRAPE MARC.

THE TOMME DE SAVOIE IS A RUSTIC CHEESE, MADE FROM SKIM MILK, THE MILK CREAM THEN USED TO A FARM-STYLE BUTTER AT THE SAME TIME.

TODAY IT BENEFITS FROM A PGI WHICH SUPERVISES ITS DEVELOPMENT AND PROTECTS IT FROM COUNTERFEITS. THE MENTION SAVOY ON THE TOP OR THE HEEL OF THE TOMME MAKES IT POSSIBLE TO DIFFERENTIATE IT FROM OTHER MOUNTAIN TOMMES.

STEPS OF PRODUCTION
Seeding, aging, coagulation (rennet), slicing and stirring of the curd, moulding, pressing then draining with flipping, salting with dry salt or in brine. Maturation in warm cellars (8 to 13 °C), from 1 to 3 months.

CUTTING

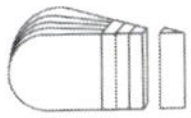

First cut the tip, then slices parallel to the crust. From half-way up the portion, cutting is done in vertical slices including crust.

BEST TASTING PERIOD
August to February.

SERVING
At room temperature, remove it from the refrigerator 1 hour before tasting.

STORAGE
In the refrigerator's crisper, packaged in its original paper or in a rag.

COOKED PRESSED CHEESE

REGIONE
Chablais, Haute-Savoie.

MILK AND FEEDING
Raw cow's milk, whole. Cows: Abondance, Tarentaise, Montbéliarde. Fodder from the appellation area and pastures of 150 days.

APPEARANCE
Soft and melting, ivory to pale yellow in colour; Golden yellow to brown crust.

TASTE AND FLAVOUR
Fine and strong, lightly salted, fruity flavour, nutty notes, touch of bitterness, long in the mouth.

ACCOMPANIMENTS
Cereal bread, country bread, walnut bread, apple, pear, fresh pineapple, dried or as a jam, white grape, walnut, hazelnut.

WINES
A white from Savoie would be perfect: chasselas, roussanne, altesse. You might try a livelier white from Burgundy (chardonnay): chablis, petit-chablis, bourgogne chitry.

AOC/AOP : 1990/1996

ABONDANCE

IT IS DISTINGUISHED FROM THE MOUNTAIN TOMMES BY ITS RELATIVELY SMALL SIZE – 7 TO 8 CM HIGH FOR 6 TO 12 KG – AND THE FLEXIBILITY OF ITS PRESSED HALF-BAKED CENTER.

ONLY PRODUCED IN THE MOUNTAINS OF HAUTE-SAVOIE, AT MORE THAN 1,300 METERS ABOVE SEA LEVEL, ITS SLOW COAGULATION AND ITS THREE-MONTH RIPENING OFFER THE BEST CONDITIONS TO EXPRESS ALL THE FLAVORS OF THE PASTURES' RICH AND VARIED FLORA.

IT TAKES ITS NAME FROM THE VALLEY OF ABONDANCE AND THE BREED OF COWS WHOSE MILK IT IS MADE FROM.

FARM PRODUCTIONS ARE DISTINGUISHED BY AN OVAL CASEIN PLATE OF DAIRY PRODUCTS THAT ARE MARKED WITH A SQUARE PLATE.

STEPS OF PRODUCTION
Coagulation (rennet), cutting the curd with a wire curd slicer, heating the milk at 45 ° C, moulding in a circle cast, pressing 7 hours minimum, salting. 100 days minimum ripening between 10 and 13 ° C, on spruce planks.

CUTTING

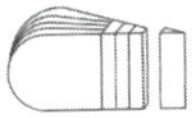

First cut the tip, then slices parallel to the crust. From half-way up the portion, cutting is done in vertical slices including crust.

BEST TASTING PERIOD
July to November.

SERVING
At room temperature, remove it from the refrigerator 30 minutes before tasting.

STORAGE
In the refrigerator's crisper, packaged in its original paper or in a rag.

REGION
Savoie,
Haute-Savoie.

MILK AND FEEDING
Raw cow's milk, whole.
Cows: Tarentaise and Abondance.
Fodder from the appellation area, pasture grazing.

APPEARANCE
Firm and melting to supple and smooth;
Ivory to pale yellow;
Yellow to brown crust.

TASTE AND FLAVOUR
Young: rich, sweet and complex flavour; chalet d'alpage: Honey notes, spicy and floral flavour, long in the mouth.

ACCOMPANIMENTS
Country bread, cereal bread, walnut bread, seed baguette, apples, pears, white grapes, walnuts, orange marmalade, deli meats.

WINES
The best pairing with a beaufort is a white: roussette-de-savoie, chignin-bergeron (chasselas, roussanne, altesse).

AOC/AOP : 1968/1996

BEAUFORT

THIS PRESSED, COOKED CHEESE WITH NATURAL, BRUSHED CRUST OF EXCEPTIONAL AROMATIC QUALITIES APPEARS IN SEVERAL VARIETIES. THE FRUITIER SUMMER BEAUFORT IS PRODUCED FROM JUNE TO OCTOBER, ONLY FROM GRAZED GRASSES, AND IS RECOGNISED BY THE DISTINCTIVE YELLOW OF ITS INTERIOR. THE PALER WINTER BEAUFORT COMES FROM PASTURE HAYS. THE CHALTET D'ALPAGE BEAUFORT IS PRODUCED FROM THE MILK OF A SINGLE HERD UP AT MORE THAN 1,500 METERS ALTITUDE IN THE ALPS.

THE SLOW MATURATION OF THE CHEESE TAKING 6 MONTHS ALONG WITH THE QUALITY OF THE MILK FROM THE HIGH MOUNTAINS MAKES THE BEAUFORT AN EXCEPTIONAL CHEESE, NICKNAMED BY BRILLAT-SAVARIN AS THE «PRINCE OF CHEESES».

STEPS OF PRODUCTION
Coagulation (rennet), slicing of the curd and baking from 53 to 56 ° C, casting in a «Beaufort Circle», pressing with rollovers for at least 15 hours, brining. Maturing for 5 months minimum in cool cellars (6 to 12 ° C) on spruce planks.

CUTTING

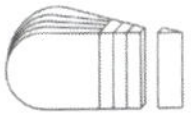

First cut the tip, then slices parallel to the crust. From half-way up the portion, cutting is done in vertical slices including crust.

BEST TASTING PERIOD
September to May.

SERVING
From 15 to 18 ° C, remove from refrigerator 1 hour before tasting.

STORAGE
In the refrigerator's crisper, packaged in its original paper or in a rag.

REGIONE
Franche-Comté, Jura.

MILK AND FEEDING
Cow's milk, whole. Cows: Montbéliarde and French Simmental. Fodder from the appellation area, pasture grazing.

APPEARANCE
Soft and smooth; crumbly and slightly crystallized if very mature; Ivory to yellow colour; Yellow to brown crust, rough on the surface.

TASTE AND FLAVOUR
6 families of flavour: fruity, milky, roasted, animal, vegetable, spicy and more than 90 variations thereof.

ACCOMPANIMENTS
Country bread, cereal bread, walnut bread, apples, pears, quinces, white grapes, figs, almonds, chives, fig or red fruit jam, orange marmalade, cold cuts.

WINES
The best friend of the comté is the Savagnin cépage. So, choose a yellow wine from the designations of côtes-du-jura, arbois, l'étoile or château-chalon.

AOC/AOP : 1958/1996

COMTÉ

ON AVERAGE, 450 LITRES OF MILK, OR THE MILK OF 30 COWS, IS NEEDED TO MAKE ONE WHEEL OF COMTÉ. IN ORDER TO MAKE THESE IMPOSING WHEELS WEIGHING 35 KG, THE VILLAGERS OF THE JURA WORK TOGETHER IN SMALL COOPERATIVES. IN THESE COOPERATIVES, THE COMTÉ IS PRODUCED ACCORDING TO STRICT TRADITIONAL STANDARDS TO THIS DAY, WHICH THE AOP GUARANTEES ARE RESPECTED.

THE PASTURES OF JURA MASSIF OFFER AN ABUNDANT AND VARIED FLORA, PRODUCING AN EXCEPTIONALLY SOFT MILK IN THE MONTBÉLIARDE COWS, WHICH MAKES COMTÉ A PARTICULARLY BELOVED CHEESE. THE ARRAYS OF TASTES AND NUANCES THAT THE COMTÉ OFFERS VARIES GREATLY, DEPENDING ON THE INDIVIDUAL CHEESE MAKING COOPERATIVES.

A GREEN CASEIN PLATE AFFIXED TO ITS HEEL ALLOWS ONE TO IDENTIFY THE MANUFACTURING WORKSHOP WHERE IT WAS PRODUCED.

STEPS OF PRODUCTION
Coagulation (rennet), heating of the curd at 53 ° C for 30 minutes, pressing for 6 hours minimum. Aging on a spruce board from 120 days to 30 months. During this phase the cheeses are turned over regularly, salted with dry salt and rubbed with brine.

CUTTING

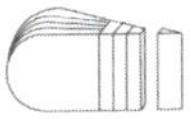

First cut the tip, then slices parallel to the crust. From half-way up the portion, cutting is done in vertical slices including crust.

BEST TASTING PERIOD
April to November.

SERVING
From 15 to 18 ° C, remove from refrigerator 1 hour before tasting.

STORAGE
At the bottom of the refrigerator, in its original packaging.

REGION
Savoie,
Haute-Savoie.

MILK AND FEEDING
Raw cow's milk, raw or partly skimmed.
Cows: Abondance, Montbéliarde, Tarentaise.
Fodder and pasture grazing.

APPEARANCE
Firm and fluffy, ivory-yellow colour dotted with holes, yellow-brown to yellow crust.

TASTE AND FLAVOUR
Light salty taste, fruity and tangy flavour.

ACCOMPANIMENTS
Country bread, cereal bread; Apple, pear, fig, dried apricot, white grape, walnut, endive, fennel, mustard, curry, turmeric, cumin, charcuterie.

WINES
A white wine is ideal, either one from Savoie (roussanne, altesse, chasselas), or from Jura (savagnin): château-chalon, arbois yellow wine, l'étoile yellow wine.

PGI (PROTECTED GEOGRAPHIC INDICATION): 1996

EMMENTAL DE SAVOIE

OF SWISS ORIGIN, THE SAVOY EMMENTAL BELONGS TO THE GRUYÈRE FAMILY. IT IS A MATURE CHEESE, SOFT AND FRUITY, ORIGINALLY PRODUCED TO MAKE USE OF THE HIGH PRODUCTION OF MILK DURING THE SUMMER AND BE PRESERVED DURING THE LOW PRODUCTION WINTERS.

DEVELOPED IN ONLY 4 'FRUITIÈRES', SMALL CHEESE PRODUCING MOUNTAIN COOPERATIVES, THE EMMENTAL LOAFS CAN WEIGH UP TO 60 KG AND REQUIRE BETWEEN 700 AND 1,000 LITRES OF MILK TO BE PRODUCED. IT'S THE BIGGEST FRENCH CHEESE.

THE REGULAR HOLES OF ABOUT THE SIZE OF A CHERRY ARE CHARACTERISTIC OF THIS CHEESE. MATURED IN WARM CELLARS (BETWEEN 20 AND 25 ° C), THE FERMENTATION PRODUCES A GAS THAT INFLATES THE DOUGH AND CAUSES THE FORMATION OF BUBBLES CALLED THE «EYES» OF THE CHEESE.

STEPS OF PRODUCTION
Coagulation (rennet), Heating (51 to 55 ° C), slicing of the curd («décaillage»), heating and stirring, pressing of 6 hours minimum, brining. Maturation of 21 days minimum: pre-ripening of 8 days in cold cellar, then refining in warm cellar. Cooling in cold cellar.

CUTTING

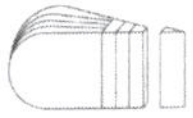

First cut the tip, then slices parallel to the crust. From half-way up the portion, cutting is done in vertical slices including crust.

BEST TASTING PERIOD
May to October.

SERVING
At room temperature, remove it from the refrigerator 30 minutes to 1 hour before tasting.

STORAGE
In a cool room (10-12° C) or in the refrigerator's crisper, in its original packaging or in a rag.

GOAT CHEESE

REGION
Provence-Alpes-Côte-d'Azur, Alpes-de-Haute-Provence, Hautes-Alpes, Drôme, Vaucluse.

MILK AND FEEDING
Raw goat's milk, whole. Goats: common Provençal goats, Roves and Alpines and mixes of these breeds. Fodder and pasture grazing (210 days).

APPEARANCE
From supple to creamy; cream-yellow in colour, fine rind.

TASTE AND FLAVOUR
Sweet and strong at the same time, pronounced caprine flavour, woodland flavours, slight bitterness.

ACCOMPANIMENTS
Country-style bread, honey, black olives, tapenade, red berries, apples, figs; either fig or cherry jam

WINES
A nice white wine with a bit of body (rich, even) will really showcase the banon: clairette, ugni blanc (cassis, bandol, palette).

AOC/AOP : 2003/2007

BANON

CLOSE TO THE TOMME DE PROVENCE IN ITS PRODUCTION AND SOIL TYPE, THE BANON HAS THE PARTICULARITY OF BEING AGED WHILE WRAPPED IN DRIED, THEN RE-HYDRATED, CHESTNUT LEAVES, BOUND TOGETHER BY RAFFIA BLADES. PRESENTED FOR SALE AS IT IS, IT IS EASILY RECOGNIZABLE.

THE CHESTNUT LEAVES ISOLATE THE CHEESE FROM AMBIENT AIR, PARTICULARLY IN THE WINTER. THEY ENSURE THE DEVELOPMENT OF AROMAS ALL WHILE ENRICHING THEM OF THEIR TANNINS. THIS PARTICULAR MATURING OFFERS A UNIQUE TASTE TO THE BANON.

IT IS A SOFT CURD CHEESE, MEANING THAT THE COAGULATION IS QUICK AND DONE WITH RENNET.

A VERY OLD CHEESE, IT WOULD HAVE BEEN SERVED AT THE TABLES OF ROMAN EMPERORS.

IT TAKES ITS NAME FROM THE BANON REGION IN THE ALPES-DE-HAUTE-PROVENCE, A PLACE OF TRADE AND COMMERCE SINCE THE MIDDLE AGES.

STEPS OF PRODUCTION
Coagulation (rennet), manual casting in cheese strainer, draining, unwrapping, salting with dry salt or brining, aging from 15 to 20 days, 10 of which wrapped in chestnut leaves. The leaves may have been re-hydrated in brandy or in grape marc, the pulp left over from wine production.

CUTTING

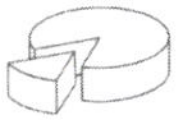

In quarter wedges or with a spoon if it is particularly runny.

BEST TASTING PERIOD
April to November.

SERVING
At room temperature.

STORAGE
Somewhere cool and dry (around 10 ° C).

REGION
Quercy, Périgord, Béarn, Aveyron.

MILK AND FEEDING
Raw gout's milk.
Goats: Saanen, Alpine Ringlet, Poitou.
Forage and/or pasture.

APPEARANCE
Fine and smooth, drier if refined; White and striated crust when young; Yellow and ornate, when more refined.

TASTE AND FLAVOUR
Sweet, hazelnut aromas, lactic notes. More pronounced flavours, slightly pungent, when more refined.

ACCOMPANIMENTS
Red fruits, dried fruits: apricot, fig, hazelnut, walnut, honey, maple syrup, bacon. Eaten cold as well as hot.

WINES
Goat cheeses require a dry white that's rather lively (sauvignon) : sancerre, menetou-salon, quincy, reuilly, bergerac, côtes-de-duras, entre-deux-mers...

AOC/AOP: NONE

CABÉCOU

THE CABÉCOU, A GOAT CHEESE FROM 40 TO 70 G, MORE OR LESS DRY, IS PRODUCED IN DIFFERENT FRENCH REGIONS.

IT MEANS «LITTLE GOAT» IN OCCITAN. THE CABÉCOU OF PÉRIGORD IS THE MOST WIDESPREAD, IT ENJOYS A LABEL GUARANTEEING REGIONAL PRODUCTION. ROCAMADOUR IS ALSO PART OF THE CABÉCOUS, IT IS PROTECTED BY A CONTROLLED APPELLATION OF ORIGIN (SEE P.122).

WE ALSO FOUND, BUT MORE RARELY, A CABÉCOU MADE FROM SHEEP'S MILK.

IT IS EATEN HOT, PAN-FRIED OR BAKED ON A SLICE OF BREAD, WITH A GREEN SALAD WITH LIGHT DRESSING.

STEPS OF PRODUCTION
Slow lactic coagulation (low renneting), slow draining, manual moulding with ladle, salting in the mass. Maturing in cellar or hâloir (10 to 15 ° C) for 10 days minimum to 28 days.

CUTTING
In half or in quarters.

BEST TASTING PERIOD
April to November.

SERVING
At room temperature, remove it from the refrigerator 30 minutes before tasting.

STORAGE
In the refrigerator's crisper, packaged in its original paper.

REGION
Poitou, Vienne, Deux-Sèvres.

MILK AND FEEDING
Raw goat's milk, whole. Goats: Alpine, Saanen, Poitou. Fodder from the appellation area, pastures.

APPEARANCE
Lightly salted, smooth and melting; White to yellow pleated thin crust, sometimes spotted with blue.

TASTE AND FLAVOUR
Tangy, subtle flavours to pronounced, goat aromas, hazelnuts, green fruits, undergrowth.

ACCOMPANIMENTS
Baguette, gingerbread, dried fruit, walnut, honey, basil.

WINES
A white wine is required: haut-poitou (in the sauvignon family), or a white Loire, from the chenins: savennières, montlouis, vouvray.

AOC/AOP : 1990/1996

CHABICHOU DU POITOU

IT IS A VARIANT OF THE CABÉCOU, BUT IT IS PRODUCED IN THE POITOU-CHARENTES REGION. IT ENJOYS AN AOC SINCE 1990 WHICH GUARANTEES ITS AUTHENTICITY AND DISTINGUISHES IT FROM THE NUMEROUS CHEESE PRODUCTIONS OF THE SAME APPELLATION. THIS UNCOOKED SOFT-DOUGH CHEESE IS RECOGNIZABLE BY ITS CONICAL SHAPE, AND ITS STRONG TASTE.

THE STORY OF THIS CHEESE CAN BE LINKED TO THE BATTLE OF POITIERS IN 732, WHEN CHARLES MARTEL DROVE THE ARABS BEYOND OF THE CITY WALLS. SOME FIGHTERS ABANDONED BY THE FLEEING ARMIES SETTLED IN THE AREA WITH THEIR HERDS, IMPORTING THEIR CULINARY TRADITIONS. CHABICHOU THEREFORE DERIVED FROM THE WORD «CHANDRU» WHICH MEANS GOAT IN ARABIC. IT IS EATEN FRESH, DRY, HALF-DRY OR VERY DRY.

STEPS OF PRODUCTION
Slow lactic coagulation (low renneting), slow draining, manual moulding with ladle, salting in the mass. Aging in hâloir between 10 and 12 ° C for 10 days minimum.

CUTTING

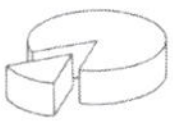

In quarters.

BEST TASTING PERIOD
April to August.

SERVING
At room temperature, remove it from the refrigerator 30 minutes before tasting.

STORAGE
In a cool room or in the refrigerator's crisper, packaged in its original paper.

REGION
Cher, Nièvre, Loiret.

MILK AND FEEDING
Raw goat's milk.
Goat: Alpine.
Fodder and pasture grazing.

APPEARANCE
Soft to dry and brittle; Fine crust, ivory to white/blue or brown depending on the ripening.

TASTE AND FLAVOUR
Delicate goat aromas (young), mushrooms, undergrowth, walnuts, hazelnuts (refined); Strong («flattened»).

ACCOMPANIMENTS
Slice of toasted baguette (young), herb bread (refined), apple, fig, red fruits, peach, watermelon, walnut, hazelnut, bacon, honey.

WINES
A white from a sauvignon cépage: sancerre, pouilly-fumé, menetou-salon, touraine sauvignon. You might also consider a lively Burgundy: chablis, aligoté.

AOC/AOP : 1976/1996

CROTTIN DE CHAVIGNOL

SMALL GOAT CHEESE OF ABOUT 60 G, FROM THE VILLAGE OF CHAVIGNOL IN THE SANCERRE. THE TERM CROTTIN PROBABLY COMES FROM THE BENSON DIALECT «CROTS», WHICH MEANS HOLE AND REFERRED TO THE ACCESS POINTS TO RIVERS WHERE WOMEN WASHED THE LINEN. BORDERED WITH CLAY-RICH EARTH, IT WAS USED TO MAKE CHEESE STRAINERS FOR THE DRAINAGE OF THE MILK CURDS.

THE CROTTIN DE CHAVIGNOL IS TASTED YOUNG, BLUISH OR REFINED, DEPENDING ON THE DEGREE OF MATURITY.

IT HAS AN IVORY CRUST WHEN IT IS YOUNG, WITH MOULD AND THEN COVERED WITH A WHITE AND BLUE DOWN WITH FULL MATURITY. THERE IS A CHAVIGNOL CALLED «FLATTENED», PARTICULARLY MELLOW AND STRONG IN TASTE, BENEFITING FROM A SECOND REFINEMENT IN SANDSTONE POTS.

STEPS OF PRODUCTION
Slow coagulation by lactic ferments (low renneting), Pre-dry on canvas, moulding and draining in cheese cloth, 12 to 24 hours with turning over. Demoulding, dry salting. Maturing in warm cellars of 10 days including 5 days of drying (+ 10 ° C). Second refining in sandstone pots for the so-called «flattened» chavignol.

CUTTING
In half or in quarters.

BEST TASTING PERIOD
April to September.

SERVING
At room temperature, remove it from the refrigerator 1 hour before tasting.

STORAGE
In a cool place, between 10 and 12 ° C or in the crisper of the refrigerator, wrapped in its original paper.

REGION
*Rhône,
Saône-et-Loire.*

MILK AND FEEDING
Raw goat's milk, whole. Goats: Poitou goats or Alpine or a mix of the two breeds. Fodder from the geographic area, pasture grazing for 120 days.

APPEARANCE
Cream ivory in colour, from soft to dry depending on maturity, flowery ivory, beige or bluish rind.

TASTE AND FLAVOUR
Hints of hazelnut; herbal flavours when young; milky, salty taste when aged.

ACCOMPANIMENTS
Pine nuts, honey, summer fruits for when it's young, apple, gingerbread, baguette, white bread, Vienna bread.

WINES
Dry whites from Burgundy (chardonnay): mâcon-villages, pouilly-fuissé, bourgogne-chitry. But don't forget about the Loire whites (sauvignon).

AOC/AOP : 2006/2010

MÂCONNAIS

THIS CHEESE MADE FROM WHOLE, RAW GOAT'S MILK, ORIGINALLY WAS A BY-PRODUCT OF THE WINE PRODUCTION OF SAÔNE-ET-LOIRE, DEVELOPED TO ENHANCE THE MEAGRE MEADOWS ON THE EDGES OF VINEYARDS. LOW PRODUCTION OF MILK EXPLAIN ITS SMALL SIZE AND CONICAL SHAPE, WEIGHING FROM 30 TO 50 G.

IT IS A CHEESE WITH A LACTIC STYLE CURD (NATURAL CURDLING), LITTLE CURDLED, DRAINED NATURALLY WITHOUT FLIPPING.

DEPENDING ON ITS AGING, IT DEVELOPS HERBAL OR LACTIC AND SAVOURY FLAVOURS, THE TEXTURE VARYING FROM CREAMY TO DRY FOR THE MORE MATURE.

STEPS OF PRODUCTION
Seeding (whey, lactic ferments) less than 48 hours after milking, curdling then manual moulding, release from mould, salting then suspension drying, aging for 10 days to 5 months.

CUTTING
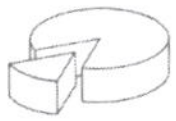
In quarters.

BEST TASTING PERIOD
April to September.

SERVING
Allow to sit at room temperature for 30 minutes before tasting.

STORAGE
In the crisper, in original packaging.

REGION
Deux-Sèvres, Charente, Vienne, Charente-Maritime.

MILK AND FEEDING
Raw goat's milk, whole. Goats: Alpine, Saanen, Poitou or crosses of these breeds. Fodder from the geographical area.

APPEARANCE
Fine, smooth, very creamy, ivory colour; Thin, pleated crust, white, light yellow to ivory, sometimes flowered with white or bluish mould.

TASTE AND FLAVOUR
Milky, sweet and long in the mouth; Young: Predominance of milky aromas, acidity; Refined: Animal, vegetable or dried fruit notes.

ACCOMPANIMENTS
Baguette, walnut bread, hazelnuts, dried fruit, honey.

WINES
If the mothais is ripe, a white wine with a bit body pairs: côtes-du-rhône, côteaux-du-languedoc. If the mothais is not very ripe, a taut white (sauvignon).

AOC/AOP: APPLICATION FILED AT INAO

MOTHAIS CHARENTAIS

THIS CHEESE, ORIGINALLY FROM DEUX-SÈVRES, IS A SOFT GOAT CHEESE WITH A NATURAL CRUST, MAINLY FARM-PRODUCED. THE MOTHAIS SUR FEUILLE OWES ITS EXCEPTIONAL SMOOTHNESS TO A PARTICULARLY SLOW CURDLING OF 36 TO 48 HOURS AND TO AN UNUSUAL AGING PROCESS ON LEAVES OF CHESTNUTS OR DRIED PLANE TREES. THESE ENSURE THE REGULATION OF MOISTURE DURING MATURATION WHILE ENRICHING IT WITH SWEET AND TANGY AROMATIC NOTES THAT GIVE IT ITS NOTABLE TASTE.

STEPS OF PRODUCTION
Slow coagulation (predominant lactic ferments) of 20 hours minimum, slow and occasional draining, ladle casting, dry salting, ripening 4 to 7 weeks (8 ° C) on leaves of chestnut trees or plane trees.

CUTTING

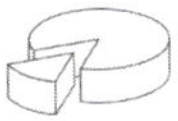

In quarters.

BEST TASTING PERIOD
May to October.

SERVING
At room temperature, remove it from the refrigerator 30 minutes before tasting.

STORAGE
Between 2 and 6 °C, in the refrigerator's crisper, packaged in its original paper.

REGION
Lozère, Gard.

MILK AND FEEDING
Raw goat's milk, whole.
Goats: Alpine, Saanen, Rove.
Fodder, grazing of 210 days per year at minimum.

APPEARANCE
White to ivory, smooth and creamy to brittle; Fine white crust, yellow to bluish depending on the ripening time.

TASTE AND FLAVOUR
Tart flavour, hazelnut aromas, dried hay, goat aromas more marked according to the ripening time.

ACCOMPANIMENTS
Red fruits, blueberry jam, honey, almond, olive oil, herbs de Provence.

WINES
A white from the South of France marries very well with the pélardon: costières-de-nîmes, côtes-du-rhône, saint-chinian (grenache, clairette, marsanne).

AOC/AOP : 2000/2001

PÉLARDON

UNDER THIS GENERIC NAME ARE DIFFERENT CHEESES PRODUCED IN LOZÈRE AND GARD, IN THE FORM OF SMALL DISCS, WITH A DIAMETER OF ABOUT 6 CM.

THE PÉLARDON IS A VERY OLD CHEESE. ITS ORIGIN GOES BACK TO THE GALLO-ROMAN ERA.

THE WRITINGS OF PLINY THE ELDER MENTIONS IT UNDER THE NAME OF «PÉLARDOU». ITS NAME DERIVES FROM «PÈBRE» IN OCCITAN WHICH MEANS PEPPER.

IT IS, AMONG OTHER THINGS, THE LENGTH OF PASTURE GRAZING OF 210 DAYS, IMPOSED BY THE AOC, THAT GIVES THIS CHEESE ITS RICHNESS OF FLAVOUR.

IT IS EATEN NATURAL OR MARINATED WITH OLIVE OIL AND HERBS OF PROVENCE OR HOT, BREADED OR ROASTED WITH A GREEN SALAD AND CROUTONS.

STEPS OF PRODUCTION
Lactic coagulation (low renneting), ladle casting, occasional draining, dry salting, minimum 11-day ripening.

CUTTING
In half or in quarters.

BEST TASTING PERIOD
May to September.

SERVING
At room temperature, remove it from the refrigerator 30 minutes before tasting.

STORAGE
In the refrigerator's crisper, packaged in its original paper.

REGION
Rhône-Alpes, Drôme, Ardèche.

MILK AND FEEDING
Raw goat's milk, whole. Goats: Alpine, Saanen. Fodder from 80% of the appellation area.

APPEARANCE
White to yellow; Firm, smooth, and fine to brittle according to the ripening. Thin crust, white and ornate.

TASTEAND FLAVOUR
A little salty and a little acidic, goat aromas that develop over time. The Picodon, so-called «Dieulefit method» is more pronounced.

ACCOMPANIMENTS
Sweet-flavoured bread, dried fruit bread, sourdough bread; Fig, honey; Olive oil and herbes de Provence.

WINES
A white wine from the South is its best friend: ventoux, côtes-de-provence, crozes-hermitage, côtes-du-rhône, pierrevert (roussanne, marsanne, ugni blanc).

AOC/AOP : 1983/1996

PICODON

PRODUCED IN THE MOUNTAINOUS AREAS OF THE DRÔME AND ARDÈCHE, THE PICODON IS EASILY MISTAKEN FOR ITS CLOSE NEIGHBOUR THE PÉLARDON. IT IS DISTINGUISHED BY A LONGER AGING AND A MORE PRONOUNCED CHARACTER.

DERIVED FROM THE WORD «PICHOT», SMALL IN OCCITAN, THERE IS A VERSION CALLED «DIEULEFIT METHOD» WITH A MORE ELABORATE MATURATION (TWO INTERSPERSED REFINEMENTS SEPARATED BY A WASHING PHASE) THAT IS LONGER, A MINIMUM OF ONE MONTH. THESE PICODONS DEVELOP MORE FULL-BODIED AROMAS AND A PUNGENT TASTE INTENSIFYING ACCORDING TO THE RIPENING TIME.

STEPS OF PRODUCTION
Lactic coagulation (low renneting), ladle casting, occasional draining, dry salting, minimum 14 day ripening. The refining time of the Picodon «Dieulefit method» varies from 1 to several months.

CUTTING
In half or in quarters.

BEST TASTING PERIOD
April to August.

SERVING
At room temperature, remove it from the refrigerator 30 minutes before tasting.

STORAGE
At less than 8 °C, in the refrigerator's crisper, packaged in its original paper.

REGION
Centre-Val-de-Loire, Indre.

MILK AND FEEDING
Raw goat's milk, whole. Goats: Alpine, Saanen and Poitou, or cross-breeds of those varieties. Fodder of the designation area, pasture grazing.

APPEARANCE
Young: fine, smooth and runny; aged: firm and dense; dry rind, pale cream in colour, blue-grey mould on the surface if aged longer.

TASTE AND FLAVOUR
Caprine flavours, notes of straw and hazelnuts. Young: acidic tastes, lightly salty; stronger flavours in the more ripe variants.

ACCOMPANIMENTS
Country-style bread, olive bread, Vienna bread, gingerbread, red berries, peaches, watermelon, apples, figs, honey, crushed mint.

WINES
Look for a pairing with a regional white wine (sauvignon): menetou-salon, reuilly, cheverny, sancerre, or try a dry white from Burgundy (chardonnay).

AOC/AOP : 1972/1996

POULIGNY SAINT-PIERRE

IT IS RECOGNIZED BY ITS TRUNCATED PYRAMID SHAPE, WHICH GIVES IT ITS NAME «EIFFEL TOWER». IT IS ALSO ONE OF THE RARE GOAT CHEESES OF THE REGION TO NOT BE ASH-COATED.

OF THE LACTIC CURD TYPE - COAGULATION OF THE MILK WITH LACTIC FERMENTS - THE FULL DEVELOPMENT OF FLAVOURS AND THE FINENESS OF THE CORE DERIVE FROM A SLOW, AND UNFORCED DRAINING. THE SPECIFIC FLORA THAT GROWS IN THE SOIL OF THE AREA (CHERRIES, HEATH, FRAGRANT AND THORNY SPECIES, AND OAKS) ALLOWS THE GOATS TO PRODUCE A FRAGRANT MILK THAT DRAWS ITS FLAVOURS FROM STRAW AND NUTS.

IT IS FOUND IN DIFFERENT VERSIONS: IN A SMALL FORMAT OF 150 G (THE «PETIT POULIGNY»), OR FOLLOWING TWO AGING PERIODS - FRUITY AND RUNNY IF RIPENED TO WHITE, OR FIRMER AND STRONGER IF RIPENED TO BLUE.

THE POULIGNY-SAINT-PIERRE IS THE FIRST GOAT CHEESE TO HAVE RECEIVED AN AOC IN 1972.

STEPS OF PRODUCTION
Slow coagulation with added lactic ferments and rennet, moulding by ladle, slow, natural draining, salting with dry salt, ripening over 10 days minimum.

CUTTING

Quarters, from the centre out.

BEST TASTING PERIOD
June to October.

SERVING
Room temperature; allow to sit at room temperature for a half an hour before tasting.

STORAGE
Keep in the refrigerator between 2 and 4 °C, in the crisper.

REGION
Rhône-Alpes.

MILK AND FEEDING
Raw goat's milk, whole. Goats: Alpine or Saanen or bred from the crossing of these breeds. Fodder and pasture grazing.

APPEARANCE
Ivory white, firm and smooth, creamy; Ivory crust spotted with white to blue moulds.

TASTE AND FLAVOUR
Mild, lightly salted, lactic, hazelnut, undergrowth.

ACCOMPANIMENTS
Country bread, apple, walnut, hazelnut, pinion, mescaline, fresh thyme, chives, honey.

WINES
A white from the Rhône valley (viognier, marsanne, roussanne): condrieu, saint-péray, hermitage, saint-joseph, ventoux, châteauneuf-du-pape.

AOC/AOP : 2009/2013

RIGOTTE DE CONDRIEU

IT IS A SMALL GOAT CHEESE OF 30 G WITH UNPRESSED SOFT DOUGH AND NATURAL CRUST, A MADE FROM LACTIC CURD.

IT IS PRODUCED IN THE REGIONAL NATURAL PARK OF PILAT IN THE LYON REGION. IT TAKES ITS NAME FROM THE TERMS «RIGOL» AND «RIGOT» WHICH REFER TO SMALL STREAMS THAT DESCEND FROM THE MASSIF OF PILAT TO THE VALLEYS OF CONDRIEU WHERE IT WAS TRADITIONALLY MARKETED.

IT IS EATEN HALF DRY OR AGED.

STEPS OF PRODUCTION
Milk maturation from 2 to 24 hours, lactic coagulation (lactic ferments) and renneting, moulding with ladle or curd shovel, draining with flipping at around 20 to 24 hours, wiping, drying and refining from 8 days minimum to 3 weeks.

CUTTING

In quarters.

BEST TASTING PERIOD
May to August.

SERVING
At room temperature, remove it from the refrigerator 30 minutes before tasting.

STORAGE
Between 8 and 12 °C, in the refrigerator's crisper, packaged in its original paper.

REGION
Quercy.

MILK AND FEEDING
Raw goat's milk, whole. Goats: Alpine or Saanen. Fodder and pasture grazing of 80% of the designation area.

APPEARANCE
Tender and varying from creamy to dry.

TASTE AND FLAVOUR
Lactic flavours of cream and butter, notes of hazelnut.

ACCOMPANIMENTS
Sourdough, dried or fresh fruit, fresh aromatic herbs.

WINES
With goat cheeses, white wines are the most recommended: jasnières and touraine-amboise (chenin), côtes-de-millau (chenin, mauzac).

AOC/AOP : 1996/1999

ROCAMADOUR

THIS SMALL, ROUND CHEESE MADE FROM RAW MILK, ABOUT 35 G ON AVERAGE, BELONGS TO THE «CABÉCOUS» FAMILY, WHICH MEANS SMALL GOAT CHEESE IN OCCITAN.

IT CARRIES THE NAME OF A LITTLE VILLAGE IN THE CAUSSES DU QUERCY, SITUATED ALONG THE ROUTE OF SANTIAGO DE COMPOSTELA.

IT IS ONE OF THE OLDEST PRODUCTS OF THE REGION AND APPEARS IN WRITINGS FROM THE 15TH CENTURY, REFERRED TO AS ONE OF THE BENEFITS OF SHARECROPPING.

IT IS EATEN JUST AS WELL FRESH OR DRY, OR EVEN HOT ON A PIECE OF TOASTED COUNTRY-STYLE BREAD. TASTE IT FROM APRIL TO SEPTEMBER TO TAKE ADVANTAGE OF ITS BEST TASTE.

STEPS OF PRODUCTION
Seeding by addition of whey (milk), coagulation for 24 hours, draining for 24 hours, brewing then salting, moulding then aging from 6 to 15 days, the cheeses are wiped and flipped each day.

CUTTING

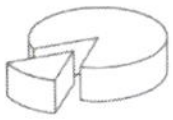

In quarters.

BEST TASTING PERIOD
April to September.

SERVING
Allow to sit at room temperature for 30 minutes before tasting.

STORAGE
In the crisper, in original packaging.

REGION
Indre, Indre-et-Loire, Loir-et-Cher, Vienne.

MILK AND FEEDING
Raw goat's milk, whole. Goats: Alpine, Saanen, Poitou.
Fodder from the appellation area, pasture grazing.

APPEARANCE
Smooth to dry or crumbling according to ripeness; Ash crust, flowered, fine, light grey to bluish grey.

TASTE AND FLAVOUR
Little bit salty, low acidity, lactic taste, dried fruit aromas, hay notes.

ACCOMPANIMENTS
Baguette and bread with seeds (sesame, flax, sunflower, etc.), fig.

WINES
Go for a dry white from the Loire region (chenin, sauvignon, chardonnay). Your options are quite varied, then: saumur, cheverny, touraine ambroise, coteaux-du-vendômois.

AOC/AOP : 1990/1996

SAINTE-MAURE DE TOURAINE

THIS IS CERTAINLY ONE OF THE BEST KNOWN AND MOST BELOVED GOAT CHEESES.

ORIGINALLY PRODUCED ON THE PLATEAU OF SAINTE-MAURE-DE-TOURAINE, A REGION WHERE THE GOAT FARMING TRADITION IS STRONGLY ROOTED. THIS ASH LOG CHEESE IS DISTINGUISHED BY THE RYE STRAW WHICH CROSSES ITS CENTRE, ENGRAVED BY THE NAME OF THE PRODUCER, ATTESTING TO ITS AUTHENTICITY. IT WAS USED TO CONSOLIDATE THE STILL FRAGILE CURD, DURING THE DIFFERENT STAGES OF PRODUCTION. THE SAINTE-MAURE DE TOURAINE IS FOUND IN THREE DIFFERENT DEGREES OF REFINEMENT: SOFT, HALF-REFINED OR REFINED.

STEPS OF PRODUCTION
Slow lactic coagulation (low rennet), hand-moulding with ladle, slow occasional drainage (48 hours), dry salt added with charcoal ash, 10-day refining for soft, 2-3 weeks for half-refined, more than 3 weeks for refined.

CUTTING

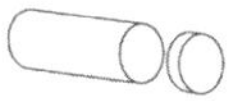

Remove the straw and cut into slices.

BEST TASTING PERIOD
April to August.

SERVING
At room temperature, remove it from the refrigerator 30 minutes before tasting.

STORAGE
Between 4 and 6 °C, in the refrigerator's crisper, wrapped up well so it doesn't dry out.

REGION
Loir-et-Cher.

MILK AND FEEDING
Raw goat's milk, whole. Goats: Alpine, Saanen or mixes of the two races. Fodder from 75% of the appellation area.

APPEARANCE
White, fresh, smooth and melting; Fine crust, ash grey, blue spots according to refinement.

TASTE AND FLAVOUR
Goat aromas, notes of mushrooms; Salty taste, bitterness more or less pronounced, tart to mild depending on the time of ripening.

ACCOMPANIMENTS
Sweet-flavoured breads like a baguette, red fruits, fresh or dried fig, dry apricot, sesame seed, pine nuts, honey, chives, basil.

WINES
A white wine is necessary. Rather lively, a wide choice (sauvignon, chardonnay): sancerre, pouilly-fumé, reuilly, quincy, cour-cheverny, bourgogne aligoté.

AOC/AOP : 1975/1996

SELLES-SUR-CHER

OF A FLAT AND TRUNCATED SHAPE, THIS SOFT CHEESE, MADE IN THE SOUTH OF THE LOIRE, BELONGS TO THE FAMILY OF ASHED GOAT CHEESES.

ORIGINALLY USED AS A CONSERVATION TECHNIQUE, ASHING – CHARCOAL-BASED – PROVIDES A FLAVOUR SUPPLEMENT AND A TASTE TYPICAL OF THIS PRODUCTION STYLE.

IT IS EATEN PREFERABLY WITH THE CRUST, AND REACHES ITS PERFECT MATURITY AT 3 WEEKS OF RIPENING, IT IS THEN GOOEY WITH WELL DEVELOPED AND BALANCED AROMAS.

FOR A LONG TIME LIMITED ONLY TO A FARM CONSUMPTION, A WIDER DISTRIBUTION OF THE SELLES-SUR-CHER HAS GRADUALLY DEVELOPED THANKS TO THE «POULTRY SELLERS», WHICH COLLECTED THE FARMERS' PRODUCTS TO DISTRIBUTE THEM IN THE REGIONAL MARKETS. THE VILLAGE OF SELLES-SUR-CHER WHERE THE LOCAL PRODUCTS WERE TRADED, GAVE IT ITS NAME.

STEPS OF PRODUCTION
Slow lactic coagulation (low rennet), slow draining, manual moulding with ladle, salting in the mass. Maturing in hâloir (10 to 15 ° C) for 10 days minimum.

CUTTING

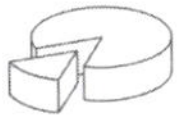

In quarters.

BEST TASTING PERIOD
April to August.

SERVING
At room temperature, remove it from the refrigerator 30 to 40 minutes before tasting.

STORAGE
Between 6 and 12 °C, in the refrigerator's crisper, packaged in its original paper.

REGION
Provence-Alpes-Côte d'Azur, Alpes de Haute-Provence.

MILK AND FEEDING
Raw goat's milk. Goats: no particular breed specified. Fodder, grazing.

APPEARANCE
White and shiny, creamy, runny texture; fine and soft rind, from brown to ash-covered.

TASTE AND FLAVOUR
Pronounced caprine taste, spicy flavours, light acidity, notes of nut.

ACCOMPANIMENTS
Baguette, bread with dried fruit, gingerbread, summer fruits (red berries, peaches, etc.), apples, figs, honey, herbes de Provence.

WINES
White wine (red, with its tannins, would bring an iron-like taste to the cheese, very unpalatable): gros et petit manseng, vermentino, savagnin.

AOC/AOP: NONE

TOMME DE PROVENCE

THE TOMME DE PROVENCE OR 'OLD-STYLE TOMME' IS A PROVENÇAL CHEESE WITH A VERY OLD HISTORY GOING AS FAR BACK AS THE NEOLITHIC ERA, THE MOMENT WHEN GOATS WERE FIRST DOMESTICATED, AS SHOWN BY THE FOSSILS PIERCED WITH SMALL HOLES FOUND AT ARCHAEOLOGICAL SITES.

THIS GOAT'S CHEESE, WITH A SOFT CURD - MADE FROM RAPID COAGULATION THAT SUITS A HOT, DRY CLIMATE - IS PARTICULARLY CREAMY, SOMETIMES RUNNY, WITH A PRONOUNCED CAPRINE TASTE AND SPICY FLAVOURS.

IT IS IMPORTANT TO NOTE IS THAT WHILE THE TOMME DE PROVENCE DOES NOT HAVE AN AOC, IT IS LARGELY PRODUCED BY THE MAKERS OF BANON, A VERY SIMILAR CHEESE, AND THUS BENEFITS FROM THE SPECIFICATION REQUIREMENTS OF THAT.

STEPS OF PRODUCTION
Coagulation (lactic ferments, rennet), slicing of the curd, stewing and draining, moulding, salting; ripening from 10 days to 3 weeks.

CUTTING

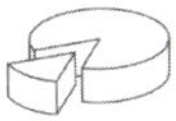

In quarters.

BEST TASTING PERIOD
January to September.

SERVING
Room temperature, remove from the refrigerator 1 hour before tasting.

STORAGE
In the crisper, in original packaging.

REGION
Cher, Indre, Indre-et-Loire, Loir-et-Cher.

MILK AND FEEDING
Raw goat's milk, whole. Goats: Alpine, Saanen. Fodder from the appellation area.

APPEARANCE
Very white; Young: dense and creamy; Refined: Firm to crumbly; Soft, light grey to dark gray crust.

TASTE AND FLAVOUR
Milky taste, long in the mouth, goat aromas, hazelnuts, fresh walnuts, dried fruit.

ACCOMPANIMENTS
As the aperitif or at the end of the meal. Bread with sweet flavours, almond bread, baguette, strawberry, apricot, mint, honey.

WINES
The valençay marries well with a valençay white (sauvignon, chardonnay). Otherwise, stick with a white wine from the region.

AOC/AOP : 1998/2004

VALENÇAY

THIS ASHED SOFT CORE, ELABORATE CRUSTED GOAT CHEESE IS KNOWN FOR ITS PYRAMID SHAPE, INSPIRED BY THE BELL TOWER OF VALENÇAY IN THE INDRE REGION.

ACCORDING TO THE LEGEND, ITS SUMMIT HAD BEEN TRUNCATED BY TALLEYRAND DURING NAPOLEON BONAPARTE'S VISIT, TO SPARE HIM BAD MEMORIES AFTER HIS DEFEAT IN EGYPT.

IT CAN BE EATEN EITHER AS AN APERITIF OR AT THE END OF THE MEAL.

STEPS OF PRODUCTION
Milk maturation, slow lactic coagulation (lactic ferments, low renneting), moulding, spontaneous 20-hour draining, salting and covering in charcoal, aging (minimum 10 ° C) for 11 days minimum.

CUTTING

In quarters, from center to edge.

BEST TASTING PERIOD
June to September.

SERVING
At room temperature, remove it from the refrigerator 30 minutes before tasting.

STORAGE
Between 4 and 8 °C, in the refrigerator's crisper, packaged in its original paper.

FRESH CHEESE

REGION
Corse, Haute-Corse, Corse-du-Sud.

MILK AND FEEDING
Goat or ewe.
Goats and sheep: Corsican breeds.
Predominantly pasture grazing, fodder.

APPEARANCE
Firm and creamy.

TASTE AND FLAVOUR
Sweet, milky, lightly salted, dried fruit aromas.

ACCOMPANIMENTS
Seed baguette, fougasse, soft flavoured bread like baguette or country bread, red fruit jam, walnut, honey, fig, pepper.

WINES
A sweet white from the South of France: muscat-du-cap-corse, muscat-de-rivesaltes, muscat-de-frontignan, muscat-de-saint-jean-de-minervois.

AOC/AOP : 1996/1996

BROCCIU

THE ONLY CORSICAN CHEESE TO BENEFIT FROM THE AOC, THE BROCCIU HAS THE PECULIARITY OF BEING MADE FROM THE WHEY, RECOVERED DURING THE MANUFACTURING OF OTHER CHEESES. IT IS STILL SOMETIMES REFINED AND SOLD IN BASKETS MADE OF RUSHES, CALLED «CANESTRES».

IT IS CONSUMED IN THE FORM OF FRESH CHEESE OR REFINED, THE «BROCCIU PASSU». PRODUCED FROM EITHER GOAT OR EWE'S MILK, IT IS FOUND IN DIFFERENT SIZES (FROM 250 G TO 3 KG).

FRESH IT CAN BE INCORPORATED INTO CULINARY PREPARATIONS, SWEET OR SALTY, IT GOES INTO THE FIADONE, THIS CORSICAN CAKE SCENTED WITH CITRUS.

THE LEGEND SAYS THAT THE RECIPE OF BROCCIU WOULD HAVE BEEN PASSED ON TO THE CORSICANS BY SOLOMON, KING OF ISRAEL.

STEPS OF PRODUCTION
The whey is heated and stirred, then salted and enriched with raw whole fresh milk and water then frothed during heating until the formation of a mass. Manual molding, draining and salting. The «Brocciu passu» is salted dry and then aged for at least 21 days.

CUTTING

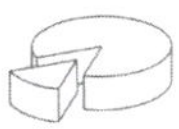

In quarters or with a spoon.

BEST TASTING PERIOD
January to April.

SERVING
Fresh at the end of the meal.

STORAGE
In the refrigerator for a few days, to be consumed within 2 or 3 days.

REGION
Île-de-France, Seine-et-Marne.

MILK AND FEEDING
Cow's milk.
Cows: all breeds.
Feeding: All types.

APPEARANCE
Air foam, light, white.

TASTE AND FLAVOUR
Sweet, milky flavour.

ACCOMPANIMENTS
Strawberry, raspberry, fresh fig, pineapple, spice, sugar, coulis, honey.

WINES
A sweet white is perfect: loupiac, sainte-croix-du-mont and barsac (sémillon, muscadelle, sauvignon), côteaux-du-layon (chenin).

AOC/AOP: NONE

FONTAINEBLEAU

ORIGINALLY FROM SEINE-ET-MARNE, THIS SPECIALTY CHEESE WAS DEVELOPED BY A FARMER FROM FONTAINEBLEAU IN THE 18TH CENTURY WHO, OBSERVING THE FORMATION OF CREAM BY THE MOVEMENT OF MILK DURING ITS TRANSPORT, HAD THE IDEA TO MASS PRODUCE IT.

RECOGNIZABLE BY ITS FINE AND AIRY TEXTURE SIMILAR TO THAT OF CHANTILLY, FONTAINEBLEAU IS USUALLY SERVED WITH FRESH FRUIT, COULIS, SYRUP OR HONEY.

THIS FRESH CHEESE, AT 60% FAT, IS MADE FROM WHIPPED CREAM ALONE OR WITH ADDED SMOOTH CURD OR FROMAGE BLANC. IT COMES IN A JAR OF 100 G WRAPPED IN MUSLIN.

STEPS OF PRODUCTION
Cream maturation (8-12 hours) between 8 and 10 ° C, the cream is then diluted with fresh skim milk and whipped. Obtaining curd by lactic coagulation and renneting, draining, smoothing and incorporation of whipped cream. Slight draining of the mixture and then canning. The Fontainebleau can be made from cream alone or supplemented with smooth curd or smoothed fromage blanc.

CUTTING
Spoon.

BEST TASTING PERIOD
April to July.

SERVING
To be tasted fresh the day of, even if it is only made of cream, up to 48 hours if it contains fromage blanc.

STORAGE
In the refrigerator.

REGION
Auvergne, Aubrac.

MILK AND FEEDING
Raw or pasteurized cow's milk. French Simmental, Aubrac, Salers or other breeds following the region. Fodder and pasture grazing.

APPEARANCE
From white to very pale yellow, pierced with holes, compact and supple.

TASTE AND FLAVOUR
Light, sweet taste, unsalted, lactic flavors and acidity.

ACCOMPANIMENTS
None.

WINES
A dry red, rather young: carignan, grenache, cinsault, mourvèdre, fer servadou.

AOC/AOP: NONE

TOME FRAÎCHE (ALIGOT/AUBRAC)

RESULTING FROM THE PRODUCTION OF THE TOMES OF LAGUIOLE, CANTAL OR SALERS, THIS SPECIALTY CHEESE CORRESPONDS TO THE FIRST STAGE OF THEIR PRODUCTION: THE UNSALTED CURD IS TAKEN AND IMMEDIATELY PRESSED. MADE FROM RAW MILK OR PASTEURIZED MILK, IT MEETS THE SPECIFICATIONS OF THE AOP TO WHICH IT IS ASSOCIATED.

THE TOME FRAÎCHE IS USUALLY COOKED, OFTEN INCORPORATED INTO TRADITIONAL DISHES LIKE THE ALIGOT DE L'AUBRAC OR THE TRUFFADE TO WHICH IT BRINGS A MELTING TEXTURE AND ELASTICITY.

STEPS OF PRODUCTION
Curdling of milk by renneting, cutting of the curd and pressing. Maturing up to 10 days.

CUTTING
Cheese cook. First cut in strips or chunks.

BEST TASTING PERIOD
April to September.

SERVING
The fresh tome is cooked: in Aligot, Truffade, in chips on a salad, in slices on a salad, in a croque-monsieur or hot sandwiches, pies and gratins.

STORAGE
In the refrigerator between 4 and 6 ° C for several days if it is packaged in vacuum seal, between 2 to 3 days if it is sold by the cut. The tome fraîche can be stored in the freezer for 3 months, cut into strips.

GLOSSARY

AOC, AOP, PGI

Created in 1925, the appellation d'origine controlee (AOC) is a French certification that ensures the quality and identity of a local product manufactured on French territory. The AOC protects the name of the product against counterfeit and guarantees the respect of a strict set of manufacturing orders, including everything from the production area to the technique and the quality of source materials. It is a tool to preserve French gastronomic heritage. The designations are overseen by the INAO (National Institute of Origin and Quality).
The AOP (appellation d'origine protégée; *PDO Protected Domain of Origin), was established in 1996 for dairy products and is the European equivalent of the AOC, which it has since replaced. Since 2009, the AOP logo or the notice "protected domain of origin" must appear on all products carrying this label.*
Much less restrictive, the European certification PGI (protected geographical indication), created in 1992, guarantees that at least one step of production took place in the original region from which the product is known.

DRAINING

This stage allows for the proper removal of moisture from the cheese, which is a determining factor in the final texture. Different techniques of draining depend on the region and the specific cheese made – softer cheeses usually need a slow, unaided draining or they are sometimes flipped occasionally to help the process along. Cheeses that are either cooked and pressed, or uncooked, are as their name indicates drained by pressing the curd, which is meant to extract the maximum amount of whey. The draining of veined cheeses occurs first during the stirring of the chunks of curd, followed by flipping once placed into a mould.

DRESSING

This operation comes in when the cheese being made is veined. The curd is ground into small chunks that are slowly stirred until they are covered in a fine film. This 'dressing' is meant to isolate the chunks from one another, which ensures the necessary aeration for the development of penicillium roqueferti, the bacteria from blue cheeses that the veining depends on.

FARM-BASED PRODUCTION AND MANUFACTURED PRODUCTION

A cheese that comes from a farm-based production is exclusively manufactured on the site where the milk is also produced. In the case of a manufactured production (a so-called laitière production), the cheese is made in a farming cooperative or in fruitières (traditional mountain cheese makers) from milk collected at different farms, all in the designated domain of origin if it is an AOP. Certain cheeses carry a label that allows one to identify which type of production was involved.

LACTIC CURD OR RAPID COAGULATION (USING RENNET)

Coagulation is the first step in the process of making cheese.
Lactic curd cheeses are created with a slow, unassisted coagulation process. The acidification and curdling of the milk are done using lactic ferments at a certain temperature. Rapid coagulation or rennet coagulation involves a sped-up coagulation process with added rennet (renneting), an enzyme taken from the stomachs of cud-chewing animals.

MATURATION

The final stage in the production of a cheese, it involves an aging for a variable period of time and the objective is to develop the cheese's unique textures and flavours. The maturation may vary from a few weeks to several years. During this stage, the rind is sometimes washed or brushed. Generally this takes place in cool cellars but certain cheeses are 'pre-aged' or dried in warm, ventilated spaces referred to as hâloirs.

SALTING

Cheeses are salted either with dry salt, meaning they are dusted with salt for soft cheeses or immersed in a bath of brine for pressed cheeses. Salting occurs either gradually over the entire mass of cheese before casting in moulds or on the surface after the cheese has been released from its mould.

ALPHABETICAL LIST OF CHEESES

ACKNOWLEDGEMENT

Sophie Greloux and Marie Baumann, of éditions Tana, would like to thank the Fromagerie de Paris (Paris, 12th) for the time, generosity and assistance they offered in making this project possible.

LA FROMAGERIE DE PARIS

ERIC LEFEBVRE
MEILLEUR OUVRIER DE FRANCE

Director of publication: Laurent Valentinuz
Translation: Charles Lee
*Graphic Design: Terre-Lune**
Editorial Assistant and Layout: Sophie Greloux